Tales of
Historic Tallahassee

By Henry Cabbage

2-20-01

Tales of Historic Tallahassee

© 1999, by Henry P. Cabbage

Published by Artemis Associates, June 1999
4303 Carnwath Road
Tallahassee, Florida 32303

ISBN 0-9667485-5-7

Printed in the United States of America

Cover illustration and book design by Lizabeth West

Foreword by Ross Morrell

Dedication

To my wife, Joan, and my daughters, Debbie and Starr, who sacrificed much because I wanted to be a writer.

Contents

Acknowledgments

I gratefully acknowledge the contributions of Lizabeth West, whose artistic talent and love of Tallahassee's history lend so much to the cover and design of this book. I've long regarded Ms. West as one of the finest graphic artists in the world. I'd also like to acknowledge Mike Hunter who assisted with researching the illustrative art with Ms. West and the Florida Division of Archives for providing the historical images for this book.

I am equally grateful to my friend and former publisher, Sylvia Jordan, for offering me a medium for original publication of many of these tales in the *Tallahassean* newspaper.

L. Ross Morrell, former head of the Florida Division of Archives, also has my gratitude for agreeing to write the foreword that lends credibility to the chapters that follow. His counsel and encouragement are among this book's most essential ingredients. I also want to thank Jim Knight, James Call and Sandy Robertson for their editing and proofreading services.

Most of all, I am indebted to the Tallahassee Historical Society for its publication, *Apalachee*, to Michael Gannon, the late Gloria Jahoda, John Hann and all the other historical scholars whose works preserve the legacy of Florida for those of us who live here and those yet to come.

Foreword

When asked by Henry Cabbage if I would write the foreword for a book he had written, my answer, although unspoken, was a resounding yes. My spoken answer was, "May I read the book and then decide?"

I had read much of Henry's writing, but all had been in the form of press releases, annual reports and assorted bureaucratic literature, for both public and state agency consumption...but a book by this guy that I worked with every day..."We shall see," I thought, and see I did!

In my nearly four decades of involvement in the business of archaeological and historical research, I have been woefully aware of my, and most of my professional colleagues', lack of writing talent for producing reading materials that are understandable and sensitive to the non-professional. Henry Cabbage has the talent, a sensitivity for the subject and a keenness of dry wit that make the following pages a treasure for lovers of Tallahassee and its environs.

Some of the stories that follow are not prideful entries in our city's past, but nonetheless, they are part of OUR Tallahassee, as are the other tales of strength, courage, romance and humor that compose this book.

> – L. Ross Morrell,
> Former Director of the Florida Division of Archives,
> History and Records Management,
> State Archaeologist and
> State Historic Preservation Officer

Prologue

Tallahassee is a city like the mythical Phoenix. It has survived a great epidemic, endured occupation, sustained great battles, burned to the ground and always has summoned the strength to arise from its own rubble and resume its station in history.

Scholars find a wealth of documents about Tallahassee and recount this city's history in the esoteric publications that serve their professions. Those of us who live here owe them a great deal for preserving our heritage. Yet, there is another set of people who live here and want to know more about how Tallahassee came to be the great city it is. The secretaries who work in government office buildings, high school students who have reports to write, policemen who patrol Tallahassee's streets, housewives who preserve the fabric of families here and thousands of others who enjoy the common heritage of the place the Apalachee Indians called simply "Old Fields."

This book is not an effort to impress the historians and archaeologists who dedicate their lives to unraveling the mysteries of Tallahassee's past. Rather, it is an effort to share dramatic tales from this city's past. This book relates true stories that lend insight about the character of the people that have lived and died here during the past five centuries. I've attempted to recount these stories with the flare of a journalist, rather than the cold detachment of a scholar. My mission is to be clear and inspirational.

Florida is a great state, and it requires a great city to be worthy of the honor of being its capital. Tallahassee is worthy of that honor, and that is the message of this book. I would not be so arrogant as to suggest that this work is worthy of its mission, but for you, dear reader, I offer it as the best I can do for you.

Part I

Strangers in the Wilderness

Hernando de Soto Arrives

Hernando de Soto, already wealthy from his conquests in Central America, wanted more. He sought greater riches and glory in the place named "La Florida," (The Flowery Land) by Ponce de Leon.

After landing at Tampa Bay May 25, 1539, de Soto brought his army of 600-700 (including two women), 220 horses, a drove of pigs and supplies to modern-day Tallahassee. The hoard made its way northward and tried to cross the Aucilla River (probably where U.S. 27 crosses the river today, according to *Hernando De Soto and the Indians of Florida*, by Jerald Milanich and Charles Hudson), under attack by the Apalachee Indians Oct. 1. It was Oct. 3 before the army was able to reach the river's western bank, still dodging spears and arrows every step of the way. The Indians gave the Spaniards no rest for the remainder of their five-month stay in Apalachee territory.

On Oct. 6, the army arrived at the site of a deserted Indian village called Anhayca (Iniahica in some documents). An Indian guide the intruders had captured earlier had escaped. A second guide led them astray, and finally a captive Indian woman led them to the village of 250 large houses.

Today the site, off Lafayette Street, up the hill and behind the Florida Department of Transportation headquarters, is known as the Governor Martin Site, so named in honor of former owner, Florida Gov. John Martin, by archaeologist Calvin Jones who discovered it in 1987.

It was a place where the Apalachees would torment the Spaniards for the remainder of their visit. On the other hand, food was relatively plentiful for the Spaniards. Foraging parties were able to gather corn, pumpkins, beans, persimmons, cherries and three kinds of nuts (one or two of which probably were acorns).

De Soto's army would spend the winter there, fighting Indians almost every day. The site served as an armed camp, at which de Soto would base his exploration of the Gulf Coast.

Three men – Luys Hernandez de Biedma, the Gentleman of Elvas, and Rodrigo Ranjel – chronicled the expedition but didn't report much about Anhayca. In contrast, Garcilasco de la Vega, who interviewed survivors later, wrote lavish accounts of the Apalachees' incessant guerilla-like attacks. Garcilasco's account reported the Spaniards lived almost in a state of siege, venturing out only to gather food. They fought off attacks with great cruelty.

"The Spaniards in Garcilasco's account, many of them professional soldiers, were fascinated with the bravery and archery skill of the Apalachee as well as with their agility and speed in attacking and retreating," Milanich and Hudson wrote. "Apalachee military tactics were to ambush or attack small groups of Spaniards, especially in wooded locales, where the advantage afforded by the war horses and mounted lancers were lessened. Apalachee warriors avoided warfare in open settings, where the Spanish soldiers had all the advantages."

The Indians preferred to attack the Spanish while they were on foot, and whenever possible, the Apalachees used their bows and arrows to kill or disable the horses of the cavalrymen. They sometimes took the scalps of their victims and displayed them on their bows.

Once, the Indians even placed long thorns on the trails ahead of the intruders to cause pain to the Spaniards and their horses.

"The bows and arrows of the Apalachee were particularly fearsome," reported Milanich and Hudson. "Some arrows were tipped with flint points. The archers' skill allowed them to shoot an arrow into a horse

past the knee of the rider, avoiding armor that the animal might have. On two occasions, native archers shot arrows into two horses' chests, killing the animals. The Spaniards dissected the horses and found the arrows had penetrated the animals nearly their entire length."

The Spaniards forced one captured Indian to shoot an arrow from 50 paces into a cane basket over which they had placed a coat of chain mail armor. The arrow easily pierced the armor with sufficient force to cause a serious wound to any soldier who wore it. The soldiers then placed a second layer of chain mail over the basket and again forced the indian to shoot it with an arrow. Again, the arrow passed through both layers of armor and the basket. The Spaniards were so impressed with the demonstration they immediately began wearing quilted fabric, "three or four fingers thick," under their chain mail and used similar armor to protect their horses.

De Soto ordered his troops to capture the Apalachee chief, Capafi. He figured that if he could hold the chief hostage, he could force the Indians to cease their raids. The capture succeeded, but the tactic failed.

Garcilaso recounted that, because of the chief's overweight condition and some type of infirmity, the Indian was unable to walk normally and was carried in a litter – which, to the Indians of the Southeast, was a sign of reverence. When he wasn't being carried, the chief had to crawl on all fours.

The chief told his captors the Apalachees would cease their raids only if they heard the order to do so directly from him.

The Spaniards arranged a meeting with some of the chief's vassals where Capafi delivered the order, but that night, Capafi and another captive secretly slipped away into the darkness.

"They used magic," was the excuse the soldiers used to explain the chief's escape when they returned to their encampment at Anhayca.

It was at that site that de Soto's men observed the first Christmas celebration on North America. Previously, local folklore had held that nearby Lake Jackson might have been the site, but excavation of the Governor Martin Site established that was incorrect.

Finally, on March 3, 1540, de Soto and his men had endured enough of the Tallahassee area and headed northward to the area now known as North Carolina and westward to the Mississippi River where de Soto died "of fevers" on May 12, 1542.

On Sept. 10, 1543, a total of 311 thoroughly defeated survivors reached safe haven near present-day Tampico, Mexico. The riches they sought had eluded them.

The Big Game

Four hundred years ago, before contact with European missionaries changed things, the big game came to Tallahassee during the summer.

To the players, the annual football clash between Florida State University and the University of Florida would have seemed like a tea party. It was a game so violent, witnesses said, it was fairly routine for people to get maimed or killed during (and after) the competition. Sometimes people bet everything, including their winter food supply, on the outcome.

The game itself was pretty simple. Some sort of official, presumably the chief, tossed the ball into a crowd of 80-100 players at noon or shortly thereafter and nothing stopped the action until one of the two teams scored 11 points – no matter how many bones, teeth, eyes or puddles of blood it took to pay the price.

To the Apalachee Indians, it was much more than a game.

"It was an act of worship," said Dr. John Hann, author of *Apalachee, The Land Between the Rivers*, and historian at the San Luis Mission archaeological site, off what now is Mission Road. "The game was dedicated to the god of rain and thunder to ensure adequate rain for the crops."

A single goalpost, which a missionary later called "this ballpost of the devil," probably stood in the middle of a large, flat, bare playing field. Atop the post was an eagle's nest, including a stuffed eagle.

Fans didn't have to stand in line for tickets. The whole village got to go for free. Probably the only people who didn't go were the ones who sneaked around other people's huts, stealing their belongings while the game was going on, according to Hann.

The only equipment besides the goalpost was a hardened clay ball (slightly larger than a musket ball, according to witnesses) covered with hide from a deer's lower leg.

Players could carry the ball with their hands, mouths or whatever, but to score, a player had to propel the ball with his foot. If the ball hit the post, that earned one point. If it lodged in the eagle's nest, that was worth two points.

In his book, Dr. Hann presents his translation of a manuscript about the game, written by Spanish Friar Jaun de Paiva in 1676.

The Apalachee Indians at the San Luis Mission site provided 40-50 players to be the home team. Other Apalachee villages furnished the equal number of challengers.

The day before the game, a bizarre ritual dominated the players' lives. They had to keep a vigil that night – staying awake and howling like dogs from time to time. It was a sort of a primitive pep rally, but with an element of magic involved.

The Indians also had to build a fire to be used for nothing but preparing gruel and lighting tobacco.

All women, married or not, were required to submit to "touching, fondling, etc," by any man the day before the game. Failure to abide by this or any other facet of the ritual was to risk bringing bad luck on the home team.

When game time came, players took to the field, as Friar Paiva put it: "...naked as their mothers bore them, except for a little (breech cloth) with which they covered their private parts," and body paint – team colors more or less.

Friar Paiva, horrified by the violence and pagan origin of the game, later wrote that once the game was under way, "They fall upon one another at full tilt. And the last to arrive climb up over their bodies, using them as stairs. And to enter, others step on their faces, heads or bellies as they encounter them, taking no notice (of them) and aiming kicks without any concern whether it is to the face or to the body, while in other places, still others pull at arms or legs with no concern as to whether they may be dislodged or not."

Sometimes players would swallow the ball to protect it from capture by the other team.

When somebody swallowed the ball, other players simply made him cough it up by squeezing his windpipe or by kicking him in the stomach.

Meanwhile, somebody stood by with buckets of water to revive any players who lost consciousness during the game.

Players enjoyed lofty status in the community. In fact, prowess in the game provided warriors a way to gain prestige during peace time. In that sense, and considering the violent nature of the game and the stakes involved, the game literally served as a substitute for war. That may have been one reason missionaries tolerated the game for a while.

Victory meant everything when the game was on. Occasionally, players even made a rancid stew of dead animals and clay to smear over their bodies to make themselves smell so foul the other team's players would lose their magic and pass out from being around them, and sometimes it worked.

One village would challenge another to the game (which Spanish missionaries later called "*juego de pelota*" – or in English, "the ball game") by sending a runner to it, dressed as a raccoon with horns. His face was painted red and his body black with red streaks. If the village accepted the challenge, the runner returned with great commotion, sounding rattles, bells and other noisemakers. If the village declined the challenge, the runner slinked back quietly.

Some of the players evidently didn't really like the game all that much, according to Dr. Hann. He said villagers made playing the game worth their while by planting their fields for them and building their houses. Village officials winked at the players' misconduct. Villagers also gave talented players gifts to use for betting on the outcome of the game.

Although missionaries eventually were able to convince the Apalachees to abandon the pagan rituals associated with the game, it is uncertain whether the Apalachees continued to play it after church officials banned it in 1676. There is some evidence they may have continued to play, in that government and church authorities announced additional prohibitions against the game in subsequent years.

The big game was a source of glory and of humiliation for the people who lived in the place that was to become Tallahassee. Individuals won and lost fortunes in a single afternoon. Brutal as the game was, it did, for a time, take the place of war. Any game that could do that must have really been something to see.

A Time of Tears

Five Apalachee Indians boarded Spanish ships, bound for Cuba in 1764, and the once-great tribe slid farther into the jaws of extinction. The end seemed too quiet for the proud tribe that had ruled the area around modern-day Tallahassee.

One estimate in 1517, although probably exaggerated, reported a population of 100,000 Apalachees between the Aucilla River and a point slightly west of the Ochlockonee River and northward into southern Georgia.

Then came the Europeans with their diseases, firepower and slavery. "Christianization of the natives" was the Europeans' cause; cruel systematic genocide would be their legacy.

According to historian John Hann, the Apalachee population had dropped to 25,000 by the year 1600. The Apalachees, despite their great courage, had not developed the art of war like the Europeans had. Besides that, the Indians had no resistance to the European diseases that spread rapidly and lethally among the native Americans.

After the spring of 1704, the tribe was so close to extinction no Apalachees were left in the land that had been theirs. Some returned later, but most of them died out shortly thereafter. Others migrated to Pensacola and Mobile or to South Carolina or to the east, but they too fell prey to fevers, massacre and slavery.

Eventually, the only Apalachee blood that remained merged with the blood of the Creeks and Seminoles – the tribes that did manage to survive Christianization at the hands of the Europeans. Yet, Hann noted in his book the Apalachees that fled to points west were able to maintain their tribal identity into the 1800s and may yet have ancestors between Alabama and Texas.

Col. James Moore, possibly a son of the Irish rebel Roger Moore, was the man who delivered the death blow. He mounted an expedition against the Apalachees in 1703. It was a horrendous bloodbath. One historian called it "the greatest slave raid ever to occur in the South, or probably in the United States, with the possible exception of de Soto's entrata (entry)."

Hann wrote that Moore's attackers swooped down on the Apalachees, killing hundreds of Indians and enslaving perhaps thousands. One by one, Apalachee villages fell or surrendered amid Moore's advance.

Ivitachuco...Ayubale...Ocula...Petale and the others succumbed. Besides those killed and captured, another 2,000 Apalachees fled into exile to protect their lives and freedom. More than three dozen villages and Spanish ranches lay in ashes as the British troops crushed the Apalachee nation.

In June, Moore brought his troops, including 400 Indians, to San Luis (at the place now called Tallahassee). Although Florida belonged to the Spanish, the British were inclined to mount military operations here from time to time. In fact, Moore had torched St. Augustine – but failed to capture the fort there – earlier that year.

Moore's invasion came at a time when many of the Apalachees already were disenchanted with the harsh treatment and land confiscation they suffered at the hands of Spanish settlers and friars. Some of the Indians defected to Moore's invaders.

Meanwhile, the Spanish set fire to the San Luis Mission, at modern-

day Ocala Road and Mission Road, to prevent the village and its structures from falling into the hands of the British. It was at that point most of the villagers fled to the west.

After that day, the fallen Apalachee villages remained deserted, used only as campsites by Spanish expeditions passing through the region. Only two villages at St. Marks reappeared as Apalachee settlements in the tribe's former territory, despite Spanish efforts to resettle the remnant population in the region during the mid-1800s.

Occasionally, Creek ancestors of the Seminoles also passed through the area after the Apalachees' destruction and visited the St. Marks settlements, sometimes simply to take scalps.

The Apalachees had been destroyed. They had lost the will and the means to defend the life that had been theirs for so many centuries. Hann reflects on that in his book: "In view of the character they demonstrated from the time of their contact with the (Panfilo de) Narvaez and (Hernando) de Soto expeditions (in 1528 and 1539 respectively) to the early years of their exile after 1704, the Apalachee deserved a better fate than dispersion and death as a distinct people. Despite the harsh reception they gave to the first Europeans who intruded on their territory, they appear to have been a hospitable people. When the Spaniards spoke of them it was almost invariably in tones of admiration for their qualities."

Today, all that bears the proud name of Apalachee is a mountain chain, a bay, a few rivers and a handful of other memorials. Only the archaeological sites around Tallahassee share any of the secrets the Apalachees took with them when they disappeared from the place they used to own – the city that now serves as Florida's capital and the surrounding lands between two rivers.

Part II
Frontier Tallahassee

The Lost Volcano

For centuries, people observed a column of smoke southeast of Tallahassee, from a swamp too desolate to explore. The Indians saw it. The European explorers saw it. People even use to watch it from the rotunda of the old Florida Capitol, but to this day, nobody knows the secret of its origin.

Then it vanished at 9:51 p.m., Aug. 31, 1886. That's when an earthquake rattled Tallahassee and the column of smoke was gone.

People weren't even sure of what to call it until writer Barton Jones of *Lippincott's Magazine* dubbed it the "Wakulla Volcano" in 1882. Wakulla is an Indian word for "mystery," and that's a fitting description of the column of smoke, but it's a little misleading about the location of the smoke's origin. The best evidence is that the volcano, or whatever it was, must have been in Jefferson – not Wakulla – County. It was probably about 25 miles from Tallahassee.

The smoke was sometimes white and sometimes black and, at other times, all the shades in between. By some accounts, people could see it glow in the dark, but nobody could get to it. According to legend, people died trying or simply gave up when the Wacissa Swamp proved to be too treacherous to cross.

Sonny (aka The Round Man) Branch, a sometimes-local radio personality and car salesman, who never claimed to be a historian or geologist, set out, during the mid 1990s, to find the source of the riddle that has puzzled Tallahassee since before the Spanish explorers first spotted the phenomenon during the 1500s.

Branch researched all the records he could find, interviewed the old timers and sifted through all the physical evidence he could track down and mounted an expedition to find the lost "Wakulla Volcano." He teamed up with another radio personality, Julian Roberts (aka J. Rob) to gather all the known information about the volcano and eventually found the spot where he believes the column of smoke arose from the swamp – two miles inside Jefferson County, three miles south of U.S. 98.

Branch and Roberts didn't pan out as a team, but they published a booklet about the volcano, in which they noted that during this century, four people claimed to have found the mysterious dish pan-sized vent with the burned interior where the smoke escaped the ground. It was not the cone-shaped type of volcano found in Hawaii, but the explorers said it did seem to have weathered tremendous heat. It would be pretty difficult to convince a geologist that the smoke came from a genuine volcano. You don't find volcanos in limestone like you have around Tallahassee, but the pillar of smoke certainly did come from something. The prevailing theory, and the one that Branch eventually embraced, is that the smoke came from a burning peat bog in the swamp.

Superstitious blacks, 150 years ago, had a different theory. They said it was "the devil stirring his tar kiln." Sailors, who used the pillar of smoke like they would use a lighthouse to steer through the rocky approach to shore, said it was "the old man of the swamp, smoking his pipe."

Many people tried and failed to reach the volcano during the centuries when smoke bellowed from it, according to Branch. The swamp, with its bogs, snakes, alligators, hostile Indians, maybe even pirates and other perils proved to be too much for even the best of men. Still, Branch found that at least four adventurers claimed to find the volcano's vent since the day the smoke disappeared. None brought back convincing evidence that they had unlocked the mystery.

Branch said he found some indication the smoke reappeared two years after the earthquake, but it apparently vanished again after four years.

Branch's and Roberts' booklet, *The Search for the Missing Wakulla (Oops! Jefferson) Volcano*, consists mostly of newspaper clippings from the Tallahassee Democrat and other publications. It recounts the local tales and legends of the mystery.

During the 1830s, and on through 1886 the volcano attracted so much attention across the country, journalists flocked to Tallahassee to report on the mystery. The volcano even inspired the 1882 novel *A Tallahassee Girl*, by Maurice Thompson.

Branch and Roberts also relate another legend, that the New York *Herald Tribune* sent a correspondent to solve the mystery during the 1870s. Despite the reporter's carefully-assembled expedition, he failed to reach the volcano and died of some kind of mysterious swamp sickness before he ever returned to civilization. Efforts to confirm the story have failed, however.

Tales abound of other journalists and adventurers who struck out to find the volcano, but none were strong enough to overcome the Wacissa Swamp as long as the smoke poured skyward.

Branch managed to collect samples of rocks – allegedly fused by intense heat at the vent. He collected letters and papers from Judge A.L. Porter of Crawfordville and forester James N. Kirkland, who claimed to have stumbled onto the volcano vent while deer hunting during the 1920s. Branch recorded the account of William Wyatt and Fred Wimpee, who said they found the vent three miles from the Porter site, at a spot now covered by U.S. 98. Still, in the absence of scientific documentation, the volcano remains a mystery.

There really was a huge column of smoke that arose from somewhere southeast of Tallahassee for centuries. That much is fact. The rest is conjecture and folklore.

The Ward-Alston Duel of 1837

"Shoot the damn dog," was Col. Augustus Alston's order to his second in command, Col. Richard Parish.

Parish complied, and that instant was the last for Lt. William Ward, fresh out of West Point. On the final day of 1836, at Camp Lang Syne (somewhere near Savannah) the young soldier had presented to Parish a petition on behalf of the men of Alston's regiment to be released from service. Their six-month muster had expired, and the men were eager to return home.

The Indian War was just beginning, and Parish refused to accept the petition, according to Ellen Call Long's book, *Florida Breezes*, published in 1893. Col. Alston, seated not far off, was enraged by the lieutenant's refusal to leave and barked his order for Parish to shoot Ward.

Bertram H. Groene, recounted the story in his 1981 book, *Ante-Bellum Tallahassee*, and reported that a court of inquiry cleared Parish of wrongdoing in the case shortly thereafter. In the months to follow, however, Alston faced the wrath of the young officer's older brother, Col. George T. Ward.

When the troops disbanded and Alston arrived back in Tallahassee, Ward challenged Alston to a duel, which Alston declined.

Ward, determined to face Alston on a "field of honor," followed Alston into Union Bank one morning and cut him several times on the face and legs with a riding whip.

It worked. In fact, Alston challenged Ward at that point, and the two combatants agreed to duel to the death at the traditional dueling ground – Houstoun's Hill, a mile and a half east of town on a placid lake. The precise date is lost to historical documents, but the year was 1837.

As the challenged party, Ward was entitled to choose the dueling weapons. He chose four large single-shot dueling pistols per participant.

The rules were that the two men would stand 30 yards apart with a barrier (which neither could cross) midway between them. They would begin with a pistol in each hand and two each in their belts. The duelists would advance to within range, fire and advance one step with each shot "until one or both were dead."

The two principals took position and advanced quickly, although Alston was slowed by a previous gunshot wound. At 10 paces, they opened fire – Ward first.

That shot buried itself in Alston's pistol belt. Alston fired three times. Two shots missed their target and the third misfired. Ward fired again and missed. When Alston fired his fourth shot, striking Ward in the shoulder, Ward spun like a top and collapsed.

"I have killed him!" Alston shouted, only to watch as Ward arose and fired his third round, hitting Alston in the arm. Ward collapsed again, never firing his fourth shot.

Both principals survived and vowed to resume the duel when Ward's wounds healed, but fate was yet to take a hand in the scenario. Alston would first have to face Gen. Leigh Read in a deadlier duel.

The Read-Alston Duel of 1839

Political differences. That's all it took for two Indian fighters, who had once been friends, to square off in a duel in 1839. The weapons were hair-trigger Yager rifles at 10 paces.

Col. Augustus Alston, head of the Whig Party, challenged Gen. Leigh Read, head of Florida's Democratic Party, to fight him in a duel. As the challenged party, Read chose the weapons and the place of the duel. The site he chose was Mannington – just across the Georgia line. The date was Dec. 12.

Martyn Searle recounted the known facts about the duel in an address to the Tallahassee Historical Society in 1949. From that presentation, and from Ellen Call Long's book, the tale revolving around the duel reveals a bizarre plot that eventually claimed four lives.

Mrs. Long wrote that Read had refused, at first, to accept Alston's challenge, and his refusal prompted other Whigs to challenge him. Refusal to defend his honor exposed Read to public ridicule, and that was a disgrace no gentleman could endure.

"If I fight, it must be with the bull dog of the party," Read finally said. He meant Alston.

The general consensus was that Read was doomed to fall prey to Alston's superior marksmanship. Alston even instructed his wife and sisters to prepare a sumptuous meal for himself and his friends to enjoy when they returned to Alston's Miccosukee home in a few hours.

According to historical accounts, it was a chilly misty morning when Read and Alston arrived at the appointed site. Read had chosen to fight in Georgia in order to avoid violating Florida's law against dueling.

The rules of the duel specified the two combatants were to stand a specified distance apart with their backs to one another, and, at the count of four, turn and fire. The two duelists' seconds – Capt. Guyton for Read and Capt. Gillard for Alston – were to enforce the rules.

The count began.

"One...two...three..."

Bam

The four count never came. Witnesses said that in an over-confident haste, Alston had lost his balance and fired prematurely as he turned.

Read calmly raised his rifle and aimed at Alston's chest, and an instant later, Alston was dead.

If the legends surrounding the story are true, Alston's sisters had the bullet cut from his body and sent it to their disreputable brother, Willis, in Texas to re-use on the general.

A month later, Willis made his first attempt to avenge his brother. At the Brown Hotel where the general boarded, Willis found Read celebrating his appointment as presiding officer of the territorial council.

As Read entered the dining room, Willis raised his gun and fired a round into Read's shoulder and raced toward the door. Read managed to return fire, hitting Willis in the hand. Willis managed to wound Read again with a Bowie knife before fleeing out the door and into the darkness.

Willis made a second attempt later, firing into a carriage carrying Gen. and Mrs. Read. The shot missed.

On April 26, 1841, Willis made his third and final attempt to kill Read. Willis, thought by some to have left the country, stepped out of Michael Ledwith's house near the intersection of Monroe and One Hundred Foot Street (possibly today's Park Avenue) and fired a shotgun blast into Read's back. As the general turned to see what had hit him, he took a second blast in the chest and died the next day.

Meanwhile, Willis darted back into the Ledwith's house and barricaded himself. He found himself in jail shortly thereafter, and upon posting bail, fled immediately back to Texas.

Ledwith, convicted of being an accomplice, barely escaped execution when the governor pardoned him.

Not long after that, news came that Willis had killed a Texas doctor named Stewart in an argument about the Read murder, and an angry mob of 20-30 Texans hauled Willis out into the prairie and executed him with guns, each man taking his shot.

Read's grave is in a family cemetery 10 miles north of Tallahassee. Augustus Alston lies in an unmarked grave at his plantation at Miccosukee. Dr. Stewart and Willis Alston probably are buried somewhere in Texas.

Four men dead, and it all started with political disagreements between two friends.

Other Fields of Honor

Two Tallahassee men of great power and prestige faced one another at Harden's Ferry near the Alabama line. Loaded dueling pistols in their hands, anger in their eyes and honor in their hearts, they had every intention of dueling to the death over who-knows-what.

One of the combatants was James D. Westcott, Jr., secretary of the Florida Territory. The other was Thomas Baltzel, chancellor at law. It was roughly the equivalent of two of today's Florida Cabinet members fighting a duel, but in frontier Tallahassee, such matters weren't all that unusual or newsworthy.

Tallahassee's *Floridian* newspaper barely reported the incident five days later in an Oct. 30, 1832 story that read: "An affair of honor took place on the 25...." The journalist went on to report the duelists exchanged two shots, and "Mr. Westcott was slightly injured."

Such "affairs of honor" were above the law in the mentality of the aristocrats of early Tallahassee. To settle disputes about politics, romance or whatever, one party would challenge the other to a duel. People simply trusted God to ensure victory for the just party in matters that were beyond human wisdom.

In his 1981 book, Bertram Groene noted that dueling was a fairly frequent practice around Tallahassee until 1839, even though the Legislative Council had made dueling a criminal offense as early as 1832. The law did little more than influence the dueling parties to cross over into Alabama or Georgia to do battle.

In Tallahassee, an ordinance required that all persons involved in a duel were to serve one year in jail or pay a $500 fine, and if death occurred, the victor was to face a murder charge. Still, duels continued.

In 1833, for instance, Gen. Leigh Read allowed his political differences with another local man, Oscar White, to fester to the point that only a multi-weapon duel could end the dispute.

They agreed to meet at Tallahassee's race track. They would be armed with pistols and Bowie knives.

At the appointed signal, the two men were to open fire at 10 paces apart. If either duelist failed to abide by a strict code of honor, the other duelist's second would be required to kill him.

Bam! Bam!

The sound of two shots thundered through the morning stillness, and onlookers struggled to focus through the smoke to learn the outcome.

Then, Read and White reappeared – shaken perhaps, but unscathed. Neither was a gifted marksman. However, neither was inclined to consider their differences settled without spilling the other's blood.

They drew their Bowie knives and charged at each other. The duelists slashed and lunged and parried and fought until both men collapsed from exhaustion. By the time the fight ended, neither had the strength to flee nor the will to continue the struggle. It was over.

Remarkably, neither man was injured, but both had maintained their honor.

Read lived to duel again against his political enemy (and former friend) Col. Augustus Alston (See the previous chapter).

The concept of honor was not limited to politics. Romance also called upon honorable (although foolish by modern standards) men to take up arms against other honorable men. On at least one occasion, the Capitol was the scene of such a duel.

The date isn't clear from historical records, but historians know that William A. McRae of Key West fought a duel at Capitol Square with Algernon S. Thurston of Washington. The subject of their dispute was the love of Elizabeth Duval – the pretty daughter of Gov. William Duval and his wife Nancy.

Fortunately for the two duelists, friends persuaded them to cease before either was hurt, but not before the two had fired at each other.

Research failed to reveal which duelist...if either...got the girl.

Even when romance wasn't an issue, romantic figures sometimes squared off in duels. Prince Achille Murat himself, nephew of Napoleon and husband of Princess Catherine Murat, was the most prominent Tallahassean of his time. He lost half of the little finger on his right hand in a duel at Lake Iamonia with Judge David B. Macomb in the early 1830s.

Historians have concluded that the fight developed over a hog that one of Murat's slaves stole from Macomb. Slaves didn't fight duels, but blue bloods did.

The weapons, the date and the details of the duel are all lost to history books, but we do know that both men survived the duel. We also know that even though Murat suffered the wound to his finger, he managed to squeeze off a shot that passed through the judge's shirt. Murat later was quoted as saying it "scared out the lice."

Duels in Tallahassee were so routine journalists didn't even record the full names of the combatants or the subject of the dispute. A case in point is the duel between a Tallahassee lawyer identified only as Mr. Campbell and another man identified only as one of the Hamlin brothers of Magnolia.

Campbell died in that duel. That's, more or less, all that's known about it except that the tale took a bizarre twist in the form of an unusual coincidence according to Groene's book.

Groene wrote that Martin's Strolling Co. of Actors presented a play, *The Dead Shot*, in town the night before the duel. During one scene, one of the actors fell on the stage with simulated blood gushing from his forehead. At that point, Campbell's wife grew ill and fled the theater, terribly shaken.

Mrs. Campbell wasn't even aware of the duel to take place the next morning, but that duel ended in a scene much like the one that had so horrified her the previous evening. Her husband died the same way as the character in the play – a gunshot to the forehead. It was many months later before anyone told her, Groene wrote.

Dueling continued in the United States throughout the Civil War, but Tallahasseans and other Floridians began to abandon such frontier practices as the statehood movement began to take hold after 1839.

In retrospect, it's difficult to understand why intelligent, honorable men would challenge one another with lethal weapons over matters that seem so frivolous to us a century and a half later. Nonetheless, the duels happened – not among lower class ruffians, but among the most socially, politically and financially elite citizens and leaders of those times. Why they dueled so frequently and casually is a mystery they took with them to the old cemeteries around Tallahassee.

The Wreck of the Steamship *Home*

Hardy Bryan Croom, a wealthy Tallahassee planter, watched in horror as giant swells swept his wife, her aunt and his 7-year-old daughter, Justina, into the raging torrent a cruel 100 yards from shore. He could do nothing to save them. Minutes later, the chilly Atlantic waters would claim Croom and his other children too.

Croom had a law degree to his credit, but he never practiced the profession. Instead, he used his wealth to indulge his passion for botany around Tallahassee. He even discovered two plants that, to this day, are classified as endangered species – the Florida Torreya (*Torreya taxifolia*) which he named for his friend, botanist John Torrey, and the few-flowered croomia (*Croomia pauciflora*) which Torrey named for Croom.

In her 1967 book, *The Other Florida*, the late historian Gloria Jahoda recounted that on Saturday, Oct. 7, 1837, Croom had boarded the luxury steamship *Home* at New York, accompanied by his wife Frances, 15-year-old daughter Henrietta, 10-year-old son William, and little Justina. The party also included Mrs. Croom's aunt, identified only as Mrs. Camack.

The plan was to travel down the coast to Charleston, S.C., then to go by private coaches to Croom's Lake Lafayette plantation, where Tallahassee's federal prison stands today. It was Croom's intention to move his family there from North Carolina after visiting friends in New York.

Nothing to indicate the foul weather ahead had come to the attention of the captain or the passengers, according to Jahoda.

Some called the steamship *Home* "an elegant ship, the finest packet afloat." The vessel was a 537-ton side-wheeler, designed for river travel. She was less than a year old but already had been modified for the coastal run.

The cruise was leisurely at first, but soon the weather turned harsh without warning. On a Sunday morning, the ship was engulfed in a horrendous hurricane. The 220-foot ship struggled against the raging ocean as it approached Cape Hatteras. The captain ordered his crew to start bailing water as huge waves began crashing over the gunwales. The skipper even asked the passengers to pitch in and bail with anything they could find. The *Home* was no match for the angry ocean.

Noon came.

By then, the captain had lost his bearings. He believed he had passed Cape Hatteras and ordered the helmsman to turn the ship westward, hoping to beach the vessel before the ocean could swallow her. Although the *Home* had a crew of 40 and accommodations for 90 passengers, according to Jahoda, the ship carried only two life preservers and three lifeboats. That shortcoming would buy the *Home* an infamous spot in history.

The wind howled and the surf battered the steamship throughout the afternoon. Women and children must have screamed as the men labored in the desperate battle to save the vessel as its timbers grew weaker by the minute.

By dusk, the wind and rain had eased and the moon occasionally peered through the churning storm clouds, but the surf was not so merciful. The *Home* continued to break apart at an amazing rate.

At last, sometime around 10 p.m., the steamship ran aground, still one and one-half treacherous ship lengths from the beach.

As the captain barked orders to the crew, the men lowered the first lifeboat into the water, only to witness the terrible scene as the swells crushed it against the bow, spilling all its occupants into the ocean. The second lifeboat never even reached the water before the waves reached up to slap it against the bow and reduced the tiny craft to splinters. The third boat overturned and its occupants were swept out to sea with the others, and still the surf pounded the steamship as if were determined to dismantle every trace of her.

Jahoda's book indicates that by then someone herded the women and children to the high forecastle, the part of the ship closest to land. There was nothing else to do for them, and even that failed. The forecastle

broke loose and washed out to sea. Then the keel broke. The *Home* was left in three sections by then, and the survivors were left clinging to pieces of wreckage amid the terror of watching their shipmates drown all around them.

The Crooms, meanwhile, had been in the after-cabin during the storm. Reports indicate that Hardy Croom had left the cabin for the gangway with Mrs. Croom on one arm and his wife's aunt, Mrs. Camack, on the other. Justina, the youngest child, led the file, and Henrietta and William followed their parents. Almost immediately, Henrietta, the oldest child, was separated from her family but courageously pushed toward the gangway. It was at that moment that the ocean poured over the deck and claimed little Justina and her mother and Mrs. Camack.

Croom's heart must have sunk as he watched his loved ones disappear under the surface, powerless to save them. Still, he pushed on. Perhaps, he thought, he could still save his son.

Another wave swept over the ship, and Croom was gone. Only Henrietta and William remained alive. Henrietta had made her way to the wheelhouse where she held to its timbers for five minutes before she too vanished into the dark waters. William was the last to go. He gripped the railing of the promenade deck until it disintegrated, and the last of the Croom household was lost.

The following morning, rescuers recovered 40 survivors among the floating wreckage. The death toll was 96.

Publicity revolving around the wreck of the *Home* eventually led the U.S. Congress to pass legislation requiring that every boat must carry a life preserver for each passenger aboard.

Settling the Croom estate required complicated litigation that took 20 years to run its course. The Florida Supreme Court ruled in 1857 that although Croom owned two plantations in Florida, he was a legal resident of North Carolina and that his son was the last to die. Therefore, the high court ruled, North Carolina laws rather than Florida laws applied to the estate settlement. Under the laws of that state, Mrs. Croom's mother, Henrietta Smith, took control of all of Croom's wealth. Under Florida laws, the estate would have gone to Croom's brother, Bryan, who lived at Tallahassee.

As the parishioners of St. John's Church mourned the loss of their friend, Hardy Croom, fate was preparing to deal them another tragedy. Come June, another shipwreck would take away their minister, the Reverend J.L. Woart and his wife, Elizabeth.

Then Came the Wreck of the *Pulaski*

The cobalt-blue Atlantic water lapped its prey, one by one, off the ship's wreckage that had been their lifeboat.

The Reverend J. Loring Woart, his wife Elizabeth, and four of his parishioners from Tallahassee's St. John's Episcopal Church all met death at sea in the wreck of the steamship *Pulaski* in 1838.

Dr. and Mrs. J. Edwin Steward and their son Samuel and Mrs. Jane Taylor, accompanied the Woarts as they boarded the 687-ton side-wheeler *Pulaski* at Charleston on June 13 for a leisurely cruise to New York.

In his book, *God Willing: A History of St. John's Episcopal Church*, writer Carl Stauffer recounted the known facts about what happened to the one-year-old ship and its Tallahassee passengers. Stauffer relied heavily on the research of the Reverend W.H. Carter who was pastor at St. John's 1879-1907.

At 11 p.m., on the second day of the cruise, the steamship erupted in terror. With a blast that filled the night sky with debris, the *Pulaski's* boiler exploded, leaving her dead in the water near New River Inlet. Within minutes, the vessel broke in half, spilling passengers into the ocean.

Carter's publication, *History of St. John's Church, Tallahassee*, reports some of the passengers lashed themselves to a portion of the bow, and most of them were saved when the schooner *Henry Camerden* sailed to their rescue. The Woart party was not so fortunate. They had secured themselves to a portion of the hurricane deck and were marooned aboard it for an unknown number of days. A stone monument in front of St. John's Episcopal Church indicates that Woart died June 18 – four days after the explosion...but who knows?

It's likely the survivors clinged to the wreckage until each individual surrendered to exposure and exhaustion, and the ocean washed them overboard and into its belly.

Rescuers saved some of the passengers, according to Stauffer, but none of the Woart party survived. In all, 141 died in the wreck.

There's no way to know what went through Woart's mind in those final days, but his thoughts might have turned to his years as a student at Harvard, class of 1828. He may have reflected on his decision to attend seminary at Alexandria, Va., class of 1831. Perhaps, he pondered his decision to move to Tallahassee in the first place.

"I was compelled on account of my wife's health to leave Maryland for Florida in the fall of 1835," Woart had written in the St. John's Parish register.

We might suppose his frail wife was first to lose her life.

The frontier character of Tallahassee must have been a shock to the refined Woarts. They arrived at a time when the Second Seminole War claimed large numbers of victims on both sides, and Tallahassee citizens were inclined to be armed at all times.

Duels were common in the Lake Ella area and on a hill in the vicinity of what is now Country Club Drive. Indian massacres were a constant threat in outlying areas, and periodic outbreaks of yellow fever and malaria claimed many lives from time to time.

This was the place where Woart brought his wife "...on account of her health."

Four Hundred Christmases

Since 1539, Christmas celebrations in Tallahassee have reflected the culture and attitudes of the people who have lived here.

The first Christmas observance in North America was among the explorers who accompanied Hernando de Soto here at a site scarcely a mile from where the Capitol stands today. Just up the hill behind the modern-day Fla. Department of Transportation headquarters, 700 Spaniards reverently observed the most sacred of Christian holidays.

It was not a time of gift-giving in those days. It was a time of religious ritual. The Spaniards probably did sing merry songs. That custom was a couple of hundred years old by then, but more than anything else, it was a celebration of the nativity to them.

Christmas trees weren't in vogue until 300 years later.

A woman, identified only as Betsy, told her Christmas story in the pages of her diary in 1824. Clara R. Hayden recounted Betsy's story in her booklet, *A Century of Tallahassee Girls, As Viewed From the Leaves of Their Diaries.*

The day after the able-bodied men of Tallahassee had mustered to drive away a band of marauding Creek Indians, Betsy wrote: "Everything is quiet again; no more scares from the Indians. Mother says it is time to begin to think about Christmas....I am going make Father and Brother gifts of little bags out of rabbit skins for their shot, but I do not know what to make Mother. I saw an old Indian squaw down on the Council House Square yesterday with a dear little pine needle basket that she was trying to trade for a red kerchief around a man's neck. (I) believe I will make one for Mother. (I) will gather the needles this afternoon. But it will not be a surprise like Father's. We can't hide anything from Mother. (Can we, Mother dear?)"

Betsy had written earlier in her diary about living in a "wilderness" like Tallahassee. It was a matter of necessity and the community's character that Christmas gifts would be simple items, made out of love and the raw materials that sustained the simple lifestyle of the bold, rustic settlement.

Another thing the people of Tallahassee could do was celebrate Christmas with a feast.

"The Hutchinsons are going to take Christmas dinner with us, and we are to have a party and tree at their house that night," Betsy wrote on Dec. 10. "It is all very exciting. I can hardly wait. Mother is making me a pretty dress out of one of hers that she brought out with us in Grandmother's old hair-cloth trunk.

"I believe I am going to like Florida very much after all. John Hutchinson (a young attorney, new to town) walked home with me from the store yesterday; he thinks it is not safe for me to walk out here alone – just a quarter of a mile from the Council House."

The young man was right.

"I shall never forget yesterday if I live to be a hundred," Betsy wrote on Dec. 20.

She had stayed behind to watch the younger children while her parents visited "old Mrs. Hobbs, who was sick." Betsy's instructions were not to leave the house until her parents returned. Her father expressed his confidence that Betsy could "shoot anything that might come prowling around," in the mean time, but Betsy ran short of the pine needles she needed to craft her mother's Christmas gift.

"When dinner was on, I decided to run across the clearing to the pine grove to replenish my supply of needles," Betsy recounted.

While the little ones – Rob, Molly and Kate – stood in the doorway and the baby slept, Betsy darted out the door with her basket in her hand. The children made a game of counting to measure the time it would take for Betsy to complete her task.

"...I could see distinctly the little fingers in the doorway," Betsy recalled in her diary.

As she gathered the last handful, Betsy arose to signal the children that she was about to start back.

"I froze in my tracks with horror," she wrote.

Betsy spied an Indian approaching the house. Perhaps it was one of the warriors that had traveled through the area on their way to make war a few days earlier. Perhaps not. He may have been one of the local tribesmen whom her father had assured her were no threat, but Betsy had no way of knowing his intentions.

The young woman's instincts told her it was her duty to lure the Indian away from the house before he noticed the children and the wide-open door with the gun inside.

"I yelled as loud as I could and ran toward the road leading into the settlement," Betsy wrote. "I looked back once – he was following. Fear gave wings to my feet....I saw, like swift moving pictures, all the terrible acts of Indian massacre(s) I had heard of during the year just past."

Although she was young and swift, Betsy was no match for the Indian pursuing her. She fell, exhausted and unable to keep up the chase, Betsy simply felt helpless and struggled to raise her head and face her fate.

Fate was kind that day.

"I saw John Hutchinson running toward me....'Betsy,' he called. 'Are you hurt?' His face was pale and his eyes filled with horror."

Still unable to pick herself up, Betsy shook her head and turned to eye the vacant path where the Indian had been.

Hutchinson escorted Betsy back to her home and even retrieved her basket of pine needles.

"We had just counted to 200," said the wide-eyed youngster, Rob, who had seen the whole thing.

On Dec. 22, Betsy reported that she expected John to "speak to Father," that evening. There was mention of a proposal.

• • • •

Twenty-six years later, two young ladies, identified by Ms. Hayden only as Molly and Bettie, wrote in their diaries at Spring Hill Plantation on Dec. 24: "While the gentlemen have gone for the evergreens, we girls are supposed to take a nap so we will be fresh for the party tonight."

While it was the custom for the ladies to hang decorations, "It's such fun to see the gentlemen try to make wreaths with their big, clumsy hands," the diary reads.

One of the writers confided to her diary her hope that Harry would be the only one to seize his holiday opportunity to kiss her as she passed under the mistletoe above the parlor doorway.

The girls all had pretty new dresses for the party to take place that night at the plantation. Afterwards, there was to be a supper and dance at Oakland Plantation.

"I never saw the old place look so lovely," the diary reads. "The whole downstairs is a bower of evergreens with now-and-then sprays of holly, thick with bright red berries. The mistletoe is there too. The gentlemen saw to that."

The customary feast was magnificent – baked fowls, roasted pig, plum puddings, cakes and "everything good imaginable," the girls wrote.

After dinner, the gentlemen retired to the front porch to talk politics. Later, during the party at Oakland, the guests danced the Virginia reel.

That night, Harry slipped a ring onto one of the girl's fingers (probably Molly's) but noted that the marriage would be delayed two years while he finished law school.

• • • •

The Civil War yielded a wealth of Christmas stories too.

Bettie's diary, found wrapped in a small handmade Confederate flag, only briefly mentions Christmas in Tallahassee 1864, a time when the Union Army was crushing the last of the Old South's resistance.

A fierce battle at Marianna in September had brought the war too close to home.

Dec, 25: "Christmas Day. No news from Father or Cousin Harry," Bettie wrote. "Everybody is trying to fool everybody else into believing everybody is brave and full of hope. No Christmas party tonight."

Year after year, Christmas seasons have come and gone – always leaving behind heart-rendering stories – sometimes historic and always personal.

Christmas in Tallahassee has evolved here from a sacred ceremony among explorers in 1539 to a family-centered time of simple gift exchange to a social occasion to the commercial extravaganza it is today. Through times of merriment and heartache, the holiday has never failed to mirror the values of the people who have lived in Tallahassee over the centuries.

Part III
Great Catastrophes

Death Came in Yellow

The fever erupted in June 1841, and before it broke, it brought Tallahassee to its knees. People said it was the hand of God that brought yellow jack to town to punish the city for its wickedness. That theory offered the temperance movement an opportunity to take hold, and churches launched prolonged revivals that ultimately changed the character of frontier Tallahassee.

Yellow fever broke out first at St. Joseph (where Port St. Joe is today) but it quickly found its way to Tallahassee. The epidemic began when a mosquito alighted on an infected traveler.

Aedes aegypti is the scientific name for the insect that served as intermediate host of the virus that caused the disease. Folks called them tree top mosquitos in those days, but nobody knew then that those little vampires could bring such destruction. Even the city's nine or 10 doctors had no idea what caused the disease.

The mosquito that started the epidemic was a female. Males feed on pollen exclusively. Only females come into the world with a thirst for blood.

Three days after biting the infected person, the insect selected a second victim and began thumping the unfortunate soul's skin with its proboscis. Soon it found the rich blood that was to be its meal, and the mosquito discharged a trace of saliva as it began to fill its stomach.

Perhaps the victim swatted the mosquito, but no matter. At that moment, "yellow death" was upon Tallahassee.

The virus entered the victim's blood, and almost immediately, the blood began manufacturing antibodies to fight the intruder. Within a week the virus would be gone. If the victim lived through the ninth day, he was immune to yellow fever.

The victim probably felt fine for the first three days, but on the fourth, his temperature rose and he felt pain in his head, neck and back. He grew tired and nauseated, and his pulse dropped. As long as he was feverish, he would spread the disease with each mosquito bite.

His eyes and skin turned yellow. Then came the black vomit and probably death.

The most comprehensive look at the epidemic in Tallahassee was a chapter in Volume Eight of *Apalachee*, published by the Tallahassee Historical Society. Barbara Miller wrote the piece titled "Tallahassee and the 1841 Yellow Fever Epidemic." She recounted how the disease progressed as the summer-time weather grew hotter.

One unidentified local doctor had logged 17 services rendered to his patients in January. During the first 10 days of June, he logged 17. He logged 41 more during the next two days. By July 22, he was averaging five patients a day.

Among the first to die in Tallahassee was the Reverend Philo F. Phelps, the local Presbyterian minister.

Governor William Duval's wife, Nancy, already had died in the epidemic at St. Joseph.

On into August, newspapers referred to the "prevailing sickness," rather than mention yellow fever. It was early September before the *Sentinel* acknowledged yellow fever's lingering presence. The other two papers – the *Star* and the *Floridian* still refused to accept it as yellow fever.

Tallahassee resident Charles Hutchinson, according to Ms. Miller, wrote to a friend up North that a local druggist had said 400 cases of fever had turned up in the city's summer-time population of 800 residents.

"We've more or less had deaths every day for two or three weeks," he wrote.

During the summer, most of the community's affluent residents retreated to the mountains, or at least to Bel Aire Resort – about where South Monroe Street now becomes Woodville Highway – to escape the heat and mosquitos that plagued Tallahassee that time of year. Some went to the luxury resort at St. Joseph and awaited word from Congress about Florida's pending statehood.

Families and individuals of more modest means stayed behind and faced the horrible disease.

Within a week, the whole Wellford family of five died.

People tried everything. In a book titled *Tallahassee Favored Land*, by Mary Louise Ellis, William Warren Rogers and Joan Morris, the writers reported that residents applied hot water and cayenne pepper to their feet and legs, reduced their food intake and exercise, and abstained from alcohol. "Some took enormous doses of calomel and were said to `look like walking skeletons more than like live persons,'" the book reads.

Ms. Miller's account indicates people demanded bushes be removed to eliminate their noxious influence and sanitation standards be tightened to combat the possibility that unclean conditions might be the source of the fever.

Still the death count rose.

Newspapers ran perennial advertisements for Muffat's Vegetable Life Medicines, billed as "good for anything: in fever and ague particularly."

Meanwhile, yellow fever spread to practically every coastal town and elsewhere in Florida. One by one, territorial legislators fell prey to the disease at St. Joseph.

In an account of the epidemic at St. Joseph earlier this century, the late Panama City newspaper editor George Mortimer West wrote that death wagons rumbled through the streets of St. Joseph, gathering yellow corpses that were laid to rest in trenches.

Yellow death.

"Great God what a death," West wrote.

The Tallahassee City Council appointed a board of police commissioners who were to serve as a health board to find a way to combat the fever. The commission found no answers.

The city council could do no more than designate that the official burial ground would be the cemetery bordered by Call Street, Boulevard Street, McCarty Street (now Park Avenue) and Grave-Yard Alley (between McCarty and Call streets). Councilmen also set standards for grave sites.

On Oct. 15, the *Sentinel* published the names of 30 persons buried there between Sept. 3 and Oct. 13. Some may not have been yellow fever victims, however.

The *Star* finally reported on Oct. 27 that the fever appeared to be decreasing, and Tallahasseans were retaking control of their lives.

There was no more mention of the fever in the newspapers after Nov. 12, according to Ms. Miller's research, although she noted that Governor Duval wrote to a friend on Nov. 13 that Duval's daughters, Florida and Mary Robinson; son, John; and two servants still were sick.

With November came frost, and at last, the fever was gone. Some say the death toll was as high as 450. Ms. Miller's research led her to conclude it was more like 80. Even the lower figure was 10 percent of Tallahassee's population. Other cities, like St. Joseph and Apalachicola, fared much worse.

Yellow fever visited Tallahassee again in 1853 and 1867, but no other epidemic has ever matched the yellow death of 1841.

The Great Fire

By 8 p.m. May 25, 1843, Tallahassee was reduced to ashes. Seven city blocks and 90-odd businesses and professional offices were gone. A swift wind blowing from the south had fanned sparks from one building to another amid the dry heat. No rain had fallen since March.

The probable cause of the blaze was arson – rooted in a dispute among three men. In a 1946 presentation to the Tallahassee Historical Society, Fred Ley identified the parties as Capt. Thomas Harris who was an occupant of Washington Hall, and the hall's two owners, whom he identified only as Call and Walker. Washington Hall stood across Monroe Street from the Capitol.

Jennie Lee Allen, a young Tallahassee woman wrote about the fire in her diary which later appeared in the booklet, *A Century of Tallahassee Girls, As Viewed From the Leaves of Their Diaries.*

"I was going down Monroe Street Thursday evening about 5 o'clock on my way to Emma's," she wrote, "when I saw several gentlemen running for dear life calling `Fire.'

"I never could resist a fire, so I hurried after them as fast as my feet would carry me. When I reached the Capitol Square, I saw flames shooting out from old Washington Hall. They evidently gained great headway before the alarm had gone out."

The blaze spread quickly to a blacksmith's shop and a carriage maker's shop next door. From there the blaze jumped across Lafayette Street to the auctioneer's block and the newspaper office of the *Floridian.*

"By the time I reached Mr. Cutter's house, the Presbyterian and Episcopal church bells were ringing like mad, and everybody was flying down the street," Ms. Allen wrote. "At first, everything was in confusion. The ladies cried and wrung their hands, and the gentlemen ran about, calling to each other wildly."

A man, identified by Ms. Allen as Johnnie Hutchinson (whose name found its way into several other Tallahassee girls' diaries during the 1800s), swiftly organized a bucket brigade stretching to the well behind the carriage maker's shop.

"But in spite of everything they did, the flames spread (beyond Adams Street beyond Jefferson Street)," Ms. Allen wrote. "Only the big oak trees on Adams Street kept the flames from crossing over to the western part of town. Oh, but we grew frantic when we saw it spreading north and east. Is there anything as terrible as a fire from under control? It licks up everything in its path."

The fire continued to devour Tallahassee. Every structure between Monroe and Adams streets fed the inferno. Two doctors' offices, three drug stores, four confectionery shops, seven grocery stores, a stable, a nine-pin alley and other businesses like tailor shops, dry goods stores and others all vanished within three hours.

The fire continued down Monroe Street to cross Clinton Street (present-day College Avenue), but Two-Hundred-Foot Street (Park Avenue) prevented further spreading to the north.

Somehow, the Capitol, then under construction, had been spared.

"Early this morning, I walked down to see how it looked by daylight," wrote Ms. Allen in her diary the next day. "Oh, such desolation as met my eye....Johnnie Hutchinson came up. He had never been to bed; his face was pale except where it was streaked with soot, and his clothes were wet and torn. He came right up to me, and without as much as a

good-morning he spoke right out: `Jennie, everything Father and I have in the world to make a living with is gone – books, office, building....last night showed me how uncertain life is....May I come down this evening to talk it over?' I couldn't say a word for I couldn't move my tongue. I just nodded my head. I guess that satisfied him for he smiled and went on down the street."

A magistrate's court conducted a laborious investigation about the cause of the fire and discovered the dispute between the owners and the occupant of Washington Hall.

Authorities arrested the occupant, Thomas Harris and a cook, but the magistrate ruled there was insufficient evidence to establish guilt.

The day after the fire, officials called a public meeting to evaluate suggestions for ways to relieve those who had lost all their belongings in the fire and to determine the amount of damage. The total destruction caused by the fire was between $500,000 and $650,000.

Meanwhile, those who survived the fire offered shelter and hospitality to their less-fortunate neighbors.

On June 5, the City Council passed an ordinance prohibiting construction of any building that was not "fireproof" in the burned out district.

The day after the ordinance passed, the *Sentinel* published an article that read: "There is none of that stagnation, idle stupor, hopeless despair or brooding, listless melancholy, which might be expected after the overwhelming blow which has fallen upon our previously-embarrassed community. All our merchants, with the remnant of their stock in trade, have taken temporary stands and are busy again. Fortitude and hope seems to be written on every brow; and all appear determined to bear up against untoward fortune."

By then, aid was on the way. The city council of St. Augustine and other sources promptly sent $300. Savannah appropriated $500. In Augusta, canvassers raised $450, and New Orleans sent $730. Even Monticello sent $100, and Apalachicola sent another $200. Other contributions, some from as far away as London, totaled $3,000.

Little of the money actually went for reconstruction. Eventually, it helped fund Tallahassee's first public school.

Nonetheless, like the mythical Phoenix, Tallahassee arose from its own ashes. The old city was gone, but a much greater one had found a place to grow and to become the city Tallahassee is today.

Part IV

The Old Days

Tallahassee in the Old Days

Indians had lived in Tallahassee for centuries, but historians mark the beginning of the white settlement at April 1824 and the birth of the incorporated city at Dec. 9, 1825.

As communities go, Tallahassee wasn't much back then. It comprised the southwest quarter of section 36, Township 1 north, Range 1 west, and a strip 200 feet wide surrounding the quarter section.

The government consisted of an intendant and five councilmen, elected annually.

According to Dorothy Dodd's manuscript, "The Corporation of Tallahassee 1826-1860," published in the Tallahassee Historical Society's publication *Apalachee*, 1948-1950 edition, there are no surviving official records of the council's activities before 1860. There are, however, newspaper accounts of the early years.

Dodd notes the charter forbade any pay for the intendant and councilmen, but it authorized a clerk-treasurer who earned a salary of $57.50 as clerk and $52.88 as treasurer in 1828, and a marshal who was paid about the same as the clerk plus a commission as tax collector. Two tax assessors collected $20 each in 1832.

To finance these moderate wages, the city assessed a property tax of 2.5 mils in 1826, but not many people paid because few, if any, had perfect titles to their property. Billiard tables were worth $12.50 per three months in tax revenue – with reduced rates for two or more tables in the same room. Liquor retailers paid $5 per quarter-year, and taverns paid $3. Doctors and lawyers were worth 75 cents per quarter, and the sale of a deck of cards generated 12$^{1}/_{2}$ cents. Other taxable items included wheels on pleasure carriages, gold and silver watches and real property. Total receipts for 1828 were $782.39.

The city tried to maintain roads, a public water supply and a sanitary service and struggled to maintain peace and order. It failed so miserably, the council "was frequently and loudly abused for not performing (its duties) to the satisfaction of the citizenry," Dodd wrote.

To combat the threat of unscrupulous individuals cornering the market on scarce commodities and the sale of stolen beef – and certainly as a sanitary measure – the city prohibited the sale of fresh meat, poultry, butter, eggs, meal or vegetables before 8 a.m. except at the municipal market house or market space consisting of Wayne Square and the west half of Adams Street in front of the square. That measure enabled the marshal to inspect all meat offered for sale and to order the removal of any unsound meat within 20 minutes.

"All vendors of beef were required to present the head and hide of the slaughtered animal(s) to (the marshal) in order that he might record the marks and brands," Dodd wrote. "It was his duty to keep the market clean and to prevent loitering there of Negroes, especially on Sundays."

Citizens had to sweep their back yards every Saturday morning and put the sweepings in a box or barrel on the edge of the streets to be carted away from the city. That was to "cleanse" residences "of all nuisances calculated to cause disease, *viz.* weeds, trash or filth of every description."

Dodd notes that most households had wells or cisterns, but the city was responsible for a meager public source of water. It maintained a well at Two-hundred-Foot Street and a lower well on or near Capitol Square. The later may have been the well discovered by construction workers at the new Leon County Courthouse, and may have figured prominently in the valiant – but futile – effort to control the great fire that wiped out most of downtown Tallahassee in 1843.

Beginning in 1828, the city attempted to maintain its streets by making adult males subject to street duty. Each man had to spend four days working on street maintenance each year or pay 75 cents per day or $3 per year for exemption. For $10, a master could exempt himself and all his servants and apprentices.

When a man showed up for street duty, he had to bring a hoe, spade or an axe or be liable for a fine as though he had not shown up at all.

The system must not have worked well, because by 1835, the city was contracting for upkeep of its streets, and a year earlier, the Leon County Grand Jury, Dodd noted, presented "the obstructions and gullies in the streets of the City of Tallahassee as nuisances – disgraceful to the metropolis of Florida...the most public of these streets, and also those leading to the town being in such situation as to render it unsafe and dangerous for the citizens of the other parts to visit the town."

In 1836, another Grand Jury blamed the filthy condition of the streets for sickness among residents.

"The problem of maintaining peace and order proved as vexatious as that of keeping up the streets..." Dodd wrote.

An 1826 ordinance imposed a $5 fine for discharging a firearm, running a horse or rapidly drawing a carriage within the city, "to the annoyance or danger of the citizens."

Another ordinance, in 1835, prohibited "riotous and unbecoming conduct...such as loud and boisterous hallowing, beating of drums, kettles, pans and the like (practices sometimes used to draw attention to political meetings and whatnot)."

For enforcement, the city depended on the marshal and a night patrol which consisted of citizens who were pressed into service by the intendant on a rotating basis. Many men didn't care for the task and didn't show up for patrols.

"This was the situation in 1840, when city authorities confronted a series of public disturbances, arising from partisan politics, with which they were unable to cope," Dodd recounted. "Tallahassee's lawlessness became the talk of all Florida."

A year later, people figured it was the sheer wickedness of Tallahassee, that caused the Almighty to strike down the community with the horrible yellow fever epidemic. The devastating fire of 1843 was just more of God's wrath, some said.

At any rate, Tallahassee somehow survived all that and retained its status as capital city when Florida achieved statehood in 1845.

Much has changed since Tallahassee became a city in 1825. The city obviously is bigger now, and it's okay to sell eggs before 8 a.m. Likewise, a great deal has not changed. The community still has a problem with street maintenance, and there's a lot of "loud and boisterous hallowing," especially after FSU football victories or even final exams.

Tallahassee had a rough infancy. There's no denying that, but Tallahassee finally matured into a fine community – admittedly one that is not without its warts, but one that is easy to love.

Knights Brought Romance to 1851 Tallahassee

Dec. 19, 1851. At 11 a.m., nine contenders assumed their posts to vie for honors as victor in the first ring tournament in Tallahassee. Romance was to be the winner's prize.

William G. Dodd, recounted the day in his manuscript "Ring Tournaments in Tallahassee" in the 1948-1950 edition of *Apalachee*.

Dodd reported that the contestants identified themselves as: Knight of the Desert, Knight of the Lake, Knight of the Lowlands, Knight of Tuscawilla, Knight of the Highlands, Philip the Falconer, El Caballero de Esperanza, Knight of the Black Plume and Knight of Ocklockonee. Their personal names in order were: Bernard Ellis, Robert H. Hall, Dr. John W. Eppes, Dr. Washington Parkhill, Charles C. Byrd, Philip S. Duval, William Moseley and Richard Duval. The identity of the Knight of Ocklockonee is not revealed in historical documents.

Ring tournaments were carry-overs from feudal times of Europe. Knights would compete for honors by demonstrating their skills as lancers and horsemen. The victor of each tournament was entitled to bestow a crown upon the lady of his choice. That was the honor for which each contestant contended.

The first ring tournament in Tallahassee was sponsored by the young men of Leon County, but Gadsden and Jefferson counties sent delegations of gallant young men to compete. Initially, the contest had been set for Dec. 18, but it rained incessantly that day.

"The weather was intensely cold, and in one of those strange aberrations which the Tallahassee climate exhibits maybe once or twice in a century, the rain froze as it fell," Dodd reported. "But on the morning of the 19th there was no sign of a cloud in the sky."

The playing field at Tallahassee was a 200-yard site, across Thomasville Road from what is now the entrance to Los Robles. Each contestant was to run three courses. During each course, each contestant was to run his horse at full gallop and try to slip a ring from a hook onto his lance. If the knight failed to spear the ring at dead center, the ring would fall to the ground and score no points.

"In the first course of the tournament, the spectators twice held their breath at the bad fortune which befell two of the knights and which might have had serious results but for the cool assurance of the riders," Dodd wrote. "When Philip the Falconer, riding like the wind, was within 20 yards of the ring, his stirrup leather broke and fell to the ground. Apparently quite unperturbed, he finished the course and, to the delight of the crowd, carried off the ring."

Later, El Caballero de Esperanza barely was able to bring his horse under control when the animal slipped on the icy grass and turned a complete somersault on an incline during his run. The knight escaped harm during the incident.

"One other incident gave the crowd an immense thrill," Dodd wrote. "The Knight of Tuscawilla was riding a restless and high-spirited bay. At the touch of the spur, the fiery steed reared, plunged, and refused to start."

Dodd recounted that the rider soon brought the animal under control, but just at the moment of reaching the ring, the horse became frightened and forced the knight to abandon his efforts to capture the ring in order to regain control.

"Notwithstanding this untoward beginning, at the end of the third course, the knight was tied with three others, each with a score of two rings," Dodd wrote.

The other knights agreed that, in fairness, the Knight of Tuscawilla ought to be allowed another run at the rings because of the misbehavior of his horse during his first run.

"The knight gracefully accepted the award, but as he approached the ring, he deliberately knocked it off the hook, thus surrendering his chance to become the victor..." Dodd wrote.

The crowd roared at this gallant gesture.

After two runoffs, the Knight of the Lake claimed victory.

As was the custom, the winner accepted the victor's crown on the tip of his lance and placed it on the head of his chosen maiden – Dora Triplett of Jefferson County.

To the victor went the honor of bestowing the crown on the female he chose to reign as Queen of Love and Beauty at the ball that was to take place that night at the City Hotel.

"Never," reported a journalist, "did coronet grace a fairer brow; never did the blush of roses tinge a fairer cheek."

A second tournament took place two months later. During that contest, the Knight of Miccusukee (sic), impersonated by Joel Blake, was the victor, and honored Martha Chaires as his queen.

After later ring tournaments, the documented queens were Virginia Wright of Leon County (1854) selected by the Knight of Monteith; Victoria Bellamy of Jefferson County (1858) selected by a victorious young boy knight, John H. Hogue; Rachel Patton of unknown residence (1859), picked by the Knight of Coral Reef; and Bettie Douglas of unknown residence (1870), selected by the Knight of Malta, George Houston.

Just as the knights assumed fictitious identities for the ring tournaments of the 1800s, the ladies who attended the balls also took on romantic new identities. Some of them included ladies who called themselves Diana, Cupid, Titania, Undine, Folly, the Evening Star, Dewdrop, the Maid of the Mist, Liberty, the Daughter of the Regiment, La Belle France, Ruth, Ophelia, a Highland Lassie, a Swiss Peasant, a Gypsy, and Night. One even called herself "Scott's lovely Jewess, Rebecca."

"It is hard to say who had the best time from these tournaments and balls, – the young men and women who were the main reason for their being or the various reporters, editors, spectators and (Tallahassee journalist) Pars Fui who wrote them up for the press," Dodd wrote. "Maybe the latter. We smile at their exuberance; yet it is nearly impossible to read their accounts without a feeling of wistfulness. The tournament, with its aura of chivalry, its fair ladies and noble knights, and let us not omit its gallant horses, has vanished....The tender grace of a day that is dead."

The days of ring tournaments and chivalrous men mounted on gallant horses truly have been nudged aside. Chevaliers have vanished, displaced by young men in swift automobiles. The gallant contenders who vied for the honor of placing a crown on the head of a lady, gave way to the new breed that sometimes lacks the simple good manners to remove their baseball caps in a lady's presence or upon entering a house or even at a dinner table. Only remnants remain of the grand Old South. There was a time, though, 150 years ago, when chivalry, honor and graciousness were revered above all else in Tallahassee society.

Honor was more important than victory back then, and "lady" had a much more specific meaning than "woman," just as "gentleman" meant more than just a "man."

Ghosts Spoke Through Wills

In the days before statehood, folks in Tallahassee took the opportunity of their own deaths to preach, settle scores, ease their consciences and even brag.

Arthur R. Seymour researched county probate records of 1826 -1845 and reported his findings in the 1947 edition of *Apalachee*. Seymour found that many wills began with a sort of mini-sermon such as: "I give and recommend my soul to Almighty God who gave it and my body to the earth, nothing doubting but that by the power of Almighty God I shall receive the same again at the general Resurrection."

Then the author would state his reasons for making a will. A favorite was: "Being reduced to the confines of the grave by lingering illness...." Another was: "Having arrived at old age but being of sound mind...."

Many were proud to announce they were healthy. For instance, one such will, written in 1799 and not probated until 1836, combined the mini-sermon with the health notation. It read: "Being in perfect health of body and of good and disposing mind and memory, thanks be given to God...."

Seymour found two cases – Davis Floyd in 1829 and William Kerr in 1835 – who made out wills before taking trips because they felt it wasn't safe to leave Tallahassee.

"Knowing many exposures of traveling especially at sea, I do make this my last will and testament," Floyd wrote.

Kerr used a little more detail. "Being about to leave this place for New Orleans on business and knowing the frailty and uncertainty of all mortal beings I do make this will," he wrote.

After specifying the details of burial and settlement of debts, the departed then sometimes inserted language to keep certain relatives from getting to any of his money.

"Several persons carefully stipulated that nothing from their estates should be used to pay the debts of a son-in-law," Seymour wrote. In one case, a man was angry at a daughter for having gone against his will in marrying James Addison. He specified that the daughter's portion of the estate go directly to her five children by her first husband.

A man named Ben Chaires requested the executors of his will to pay $10,000 to his daughter, Mary Ann Burgess, "...when her husband shall die and not before." The will further stipulated that if the daughter died before the husband, the money should go to her children.

Chaires had 10 other children, by the way, but none of the other son-in-laws were in such disfavor.

Some headed off the son-in-law factor or surviving wife's future husband possibility by using the word "lend" rather than "leave to" in doling out wealth to female family members. William Harris gave land to his sons, but loaned tracts of land to his daughters who were married, and after mentioning their names and legacies, he inserted the phrase, "...during her natural life and at her decease to be equally divided among the heirs of her body."

Another man provided that "...in case of my wife Eliza's marriage, she shall be entitled to receive one third instead of the whole of my property."

Having weeded out in-laws and such, the dead could then turn their attention to dispensing justice within the immediate family. John May, for instance, left $1 to his son John, explaining that he had paid out more money for that son than any of the rest of his 10 children could hope to receive from his estate.

Seymour noted that bedding furniture must have been especially important in territorial days. It was mentioned in many wills of the time.

He also noted that the term "cattle" must have referred to mules, horses, sheep and hogs as well as to what wills referred to as "horned cattle."

Provisions for a son's education were common in wills, but Seymour found such provisions were rare for daughters. He did find one case in which a certain slave's work would finance schooling for the slave's owner's daughter, Anna.

"One feels the importance of Negro slaves in territorial days when one finds their disposal mentioned in two thirds of the wills," Seymour wrote. "Very often, definite slaves were bequeathed to a wife or child as personal servants."

When slaves were to be sold, wills usually included special requirements concerning the new owners— such as ones who will keep the slaves' families together or would treat them kindly. In other cases, slaves were to be freed within a specified time and someone appointed to serve as their guardians and protectors.

"Beginning in the 1820s, considerable attention was given to returning Negroes to the West Coast of Africa to settle in Liberia, a country of free Negroes," Seymour wrote. "In the 30 years following, some thousands of them went there from the United States. The American Colonization Society was formed for this purpose."

In one case, a man provided that his slave, Nicholas, would be freed if he were willing to go to Liberia; if not, he would remain in slavery. Nicholas' decision is unknown.

It was customary in territorial days to require executors of wills to post a bond to ensure proper performance. Bond varied from $500 to $25,000, according to the value of the estate. When the will did not require a bond, according to Seymour, "Some such documents (were) careful to state that the executors (were) acting `obligatory to the Governor of the Territory of Florida and his successors.'"

For some reason, the earliest wills contained almost no punctuation and the people who wrote them took considerable liberties with the rules of spelling. Single letters were doubled; double letters were left single and "induring" was used for "during." "Disannule" substituted for "annul," and "intermarriage" replaced "marriage."

Peculiar as the wills were in those days, they reflected the times. While they ensured orderly transfer of the deceaseds' property, wills also enabled the dead to continue to enforce discipline and family honor, even from the grave.

Provisions in many of the old wills might well be unenforceable today, but in territorial days, heads of families used them to exercise considerable control over others by attaching strings to the one thing that always has impressed Americans more than anything else – wealth.

Proctor Bought a Wife

The concept that it is sheer wickedness for human beings to buy and sell other human beings was blurred by the realities of the time for George Proctor.

On May 8, 1839, he married Nancy Chandler in St. John's Episcopal Church in Tallahassee. The record read: "a free black who purchased his wife."

In the 1946 edition of *Apalachee*, Rosalind Parker recounted the story in the chapter titled "The Proctors – Antonio, George and John." She reported that George's father, Antonio, had been born into slavery but had earned his status as a "Spanish free Negro" through service to military authorities.

Ms. Parker noted that Spanish free negroes enjoyed a loftier position than other free blacks, because Spain had stipulated in its Treaty of Cession that they would enjoy all the privileges, rights and immunities of U.S. citizens.

George grew up to become a prominent businessman in Tallahassee. He was a carpenter by trade, and a good one. He built such Tallahassee structures as the Ashenhart house and Rutgers house both on North Calhoun Street. In 1839, he built the Chaires house, and he also built three six-room houses – dubbed the three sisters because they looked alike – on McCarty Street between Calhoun and Gadsden streets.

During the 1830s, George demonstrated a talent for investing small sums of money and turning a profit regularly.

"All available evidence indicates that George did business on equal terms with white men," Parker wrote. "This may have been due to his status as a Spanish free negro, whose rights were guaranteed under the Treaty of 1819; it also may have been attributable to the exceptional character of the man."

Where would such a man find a wife in the little village of Tallahassee? He found her at the residence of Mrs. Mary Chandler, who ran a local boarding house.

George negotiated the purchase price of $1,300 – pretty much the going rate for a slave who probably was trained as a house servant. He paid $450 cash according to Ms. Parker. George also agreed to pay the $850 balance at an unspecified interest rate within one year. As security on the loan, he gave Mrs. Chandler his personal note and a mortgage on Nancy.

His timing was poor.

In the aftermath of the financial panic of 1837, Tallahassee fell upon hard times. George found himself unable to collect money owed to him, and consequently, was unable to meet his obligations.

"He soon found himself in a maze of lawsuits, the most important of which were filed by Mrs. Chandler," Parker wrote.

Mrs. Chandler's attorneys, on Oct. 26, 1840, sued George for $1,700 on the $850 note. The plaintiff also sued for an additional $900. Parker believed the additional dollars were the result of the birth of Nancy's child, who, under prevailing law, would become property of the mother's owner.

Feb. 13, 1841, Mrs. Chandler filed a suit for foreclosure of the mortgage on Nancy. Eventually, a jury awarded Mrs. Chandler $1,023 on the note to cover the principal and 10-percent semiannual interest. Jurors, however, disregarded the additional claim of $900.

Judge Samuel J. Douglas ruled that George had until March 1, 1842 to pay the judgement or surrender Nancy and other property. Mrs. Chandler, meanwhile, filed an affidavit claiming she had reason to believe George would remove Nancy from the Florida Territory before the deadline, prompting the judge to execute the levy immediately. Parker suggests that a white friend – possibly Henry L. Rutgers – had the judgement assigned to himself. Nancy was spared the fate of returning to slavery in Mrs. Chandler's house.

George's financial troubles continued to mount throughout the 1840s, yet, he continued to ply his trade as a carpenter although work was scarce. He also made an unsuccessful attempt at farming in 1846.

A few years later, word reached Tallahassee that people were finding gold in California, and George seized an opportunity to head west in hopes of finding a solution to his financial difficulties. Tradition suggests he left Tallahassee with Washington Bartlett, who was to become governor of California, sailing aboard the *Othello* from Charleston. Parker indicated it was more likely that George traveled overland from New

Orleans to California.

Some say George did send a few nuggets back, but not enough to change the status of his family. He did, however, manage to earn $12 per day as a contractor and builder and found work plentiful out west. Still he never was able to rescue his family, and he died in California in 1862.

While George was absent, Henry L. Rutgers among others served as the legally-required guardians of Nancy and her seven (or eight) children. With the Chandler judgement still unpaid, Sheriff Haley T. Blocker was forced to sell the slave family in February 1854. The buyer was Jane Rutgers (Henry's wife), and the price was $2,300.

Unfortunately, Mr. & Mrs. Rutgers also met financial difficulties and were forced to use Nancy and her children as security in their dealings with Union Bank. Eventually, three of the children were sold to another owner, Col. George W. Scott, for $2,800. The others stayed together, hiring out to earn their keep.

Not until the Civil War ended in 1865 were Nancy and her children able to escape the bonds of slavery.

One of Nancy's sons, John, later became a prominent politician and served in various state and local offices. He died in 1944 at the age of 100.

The Prince Couldn't Cook a Buzzard

About the time Florida became a state, folks around Tallahassee were delighted to have royalty in their midst. Prince Charles Louis Achille Napoleon Murat and his beautiful wife Catherine lived here.

Although the prince became a successful planter, postmaster and county judge, tales still abound about some of the goofy things he did. One of the goofiest was his attempt to find a way to make turkey vultures (he called them turkey buzzards) taste good.

The prince made a hobby of making meals out of local wildlife and whatnot. He cooked toadstools and rattlesnakes, and he was particularly proud of his baked owl with head on and his cow's ear stew. No matter how hard he tried, though, the crown prince of Naples just never could whip up a decent dish of turkey buzzard.

Bertram H. Groene, in *Ante-Bellum Tallahassee*, quotes the prince as saying: "I roast heem. I fry heem. I stew heem, bote by gar soir, hee ees no good."

There is another story about the large St. Bernard the prince kept close by to spit upon because his wife and mother-in-law objected to the prince's tobacco-chewing habit. The dog's fur, the story goes, would absorb the tobacco juice and keep the two women from nagging him so much.

Some say the prince kept a pet owl on his shoulder. The bird, if there really was one, may or may not have ended up in one of the prince's gourmet meals.

One of the most remarkable stories about the prince concerns his days in St. Augustine before he moved to Tallahassee. Groene's book notes: "Few citizens of that once-Spanish stronghold would forget the prince's habit of carrying on his affairs of business seated with a chair, umbrella and table in the ocean with the waves rolling just under the table's top.

In 1826, the prince married Catherine Willis Dangerfield Gray, who had moved to Tallahassee with her family and lived in a log cabin on Monroe Street. She was a great-grandniece of George Washington.

The prince died in 1847, and as James R. Knott's book, *Tales of Tallahassee Twice Told and Untold* recounts, the princess bought a 500-acre plantation a couple of miles west of town seven years later. The plantation house, which she called Bellevue, now stands at the Tallahassee Museum of History and Natural Science.

When the Civil War erupted in 1861, it was Princess Murat who fired the cannon that announced Florida's secession from the Union, and before the war ended, she had exhausted all her funds, property and other resources helping the sick and wounded from that conflict.

Her late husband's relatives, the Bonaparte Regime of Paris, had regained power in France by then, and Napoleon III came to her financial rescue.

Princess Murat died of consumption in 1867 and is buried beside the prince in St. Johns Cemetery near downtown Tallahassee. Twin marble obelisks mark their graves.

Statehood Came Hard

March 8, 1845. Bells rang in Tallahassee, bonfires burned, cannons fired in celebration and the city's most distinguished citizens gathered at White Oak Plantation for a gala reception. Word had just reached Tallahassee that five days earlier, President John Tyler had signed the bill admitting Florida to the Union as the 27th state.

Territorial leaders had battled over the issue for years, but at last, the Democrats and Whigs laid aside their differences – at least the ones about statehood – and accepted Florida's new role in the Union. Some had wanted Florida to become two states. Others had preferred to avoid the financial burdens of statehood by remaining a territory. There also had been a strong contingent of west Floridians who wanted their part of the territory to be annexed by Alabama.

Also, "Hopeful Floridians thought Georgia might be willing to cede a southern tier of counties to help them qualify for statehood, but the interest of Georgians had ceased with a resolution to annex east Florida some years earlier," according to historian Charlton W. Tebeau's book, *History of Florida.* Tebeau noted that the boundary between the two states never had been settled, and the right to 1.5 million acres was at stake. Indian hostilities had prevented surveyors from documenting the boundary.

The strongest argument against statehood, Tebeau wrote, was the necessity for the state to pay the costs of administration and government. Land parcels had to be set aside for education, and two whole townships had to be reserved for higher education.

"Home rule was perhaps the strongest argument for statehood," Tebeau wrote. "Floridians complained that territories were too likely to be looked upon as the patrimony of the decayed or neglected politicians of other states."

In Tallahassee and elsewhere in west Florida, the population was pretty evenly divided over the issue of whether to seek statehood or to divide the territory in two in an effort to postpone statehood until the population was large enough to make two states. That prospect would have strengthened the political clout of the South in Congress. Tebeau noted that middle Florida Whigs opposed dividing Florida in two. Residents there had just endured seven years of fighting with the Seminole Indians and sought the protection and security of the national government.

Meanwhile, Congress wasn't sure it wanted Florida to come into the Union as a state. Slavery was one of the main problems. Admission of another slave state could upset the balance of power in Congress.

Statehood for a single Florida finally won out, even though historians generally agree that Florida's population and taxable wealth were too meager to support the governmental structure of a state – even without the depression and recent Indian war that had left Florida's economic and financial state in shambles.

Nonetheless, statehood became a reality.

In 1838-39, a total of 56 territorial delegates had met at St. Joseph (known today as Port St. Joe) and hammered out details of a constitution to be submitted to Congress for acceptance of Florida as a "slave state." Other southern frontier state constitutions provided the model for the document.

When constitutional convention delegates submitted the constitution to voters for ratification, it barely passed a referendum 2,065 to 1,961. The validity of many of the votes was questionable, according to *The Florida Handbook*, compiled by Allen Morris of Florida State University's Strozier Library.

Six years after the constitutional convention at St. Joseph, the federal government finally admitted Florida to the Union as a slave state. The opportunity for admission came when Iowa petitioned for admission as a free state, enabling Congress to maintain the balance that was critical to Washington in those days. Even then, 48 members of the House of Representatives voted against admitting Florida. One hundred forty-four voted in favor.

The idea of making Florida two states did not die easily. An early version of the "Iowa-Florida Bill" included a provision to divide Florida into two states as soon as east Florida could accumulate 35,000 residents. That provision, however, failed to survive a floor vote in Congress. The whole territory only had 66,000 residents by 1845, and most of them were in west Florida. Florida would be one state, and that was that.

By March 26, the 23-day-old State of Florida conducted its first state election, and Democrat William Dunn Moseley defeated Whig candidate Richard Keith Call to become governor. Voters also elected 41 state representatives and 17 state senators, along with Florida's first congressman, David Levy who later changed his name to David Yulee in honor of his family's Moorish title, according to the book, *Florida a Short History*, by Dr. Michael Gannon.

At the time, U.S. senators were appointed by the state legislatures, and Levy resigned as congressman, before he ever served in that capacity, to accept a senatorial slot along side another Democrat, James D. Westcott, Jr. William H. Brockenbrough went to Washington as congressman.

The General Assembly, as the Florida Legislature was then known, moved swiftly to convene its first session on June 23 to establish the government that has served this state for more than 150 years.

Part V

War

Victory at Natural Bridge

War was at the threshold of Tallahassee. Fourteen enemy vessels had landed 1,000 troops near St. Marks for an assault on the Florida capital – the only capital city east of the Mississippi still under confederate control. .

It would be only a month later when Confederate Gen. Robert E. Lee surrendered to Union Gen. Ulysses S. Grant, more-or-less ending the Civil War. Still, Florida counted itself part of the war that March day when Tallahassee sent its men and boys to defend the capital city.

Gov. John Milton, according to historian Charlton W. Tebeau, was alarmed by the Union's continuing raids and the inability of Confederate forces to stop them. The previous July, Milton had called on all citizens capable of bearing arms to band together in militia companies to defend the state.

The legislature responded by declaring that every able-bodied man, between the ages of 15 and 55 and not in the Confederate service, was in the state militia.

Then came the invaders.

Union leaders wanted to capture St. Marks to strangle the already-crippled blockade-running operations that had kept goods flowing into the Confederacy throughout the war. Furthermore, Tallahassee was an important military prize in that it was the center of the most productive agricultural region in the state with the added attraction of cotton and former slaves to be carried away.

Brig. Gen. William Miller, who fought at Natural Bridge, recounted the battle in an address to the Anna Jackson Chapter of the United Daughters of Tallahassee in 1901, quoting from official dispatches of Confederate officers. Mark F. Boyd presented the general's address to the Tallahassee Historical Society in 1955.

In his report to Maj. Gen. Samuel Jones, Miller wrote: "...Learning that a fleet of 11 steamers and three sailed vessels had arrived at the St. Marks lighthouse and were disembarking a heavy force of the enemy, I reported immediately to the major general commanding who ordered me to assume command of the forces in the field."

Miller, who had grown up in Louisiana and had a distinguished military career dating back to 1845, rushed to Newport to relieve the troops commanded by Lt. Col. George W. Scott and assumed command of the defenders on March 5. The general's command consisted of Scott's cavalrymen, militia under Col. Samuel Love, the "Gadsden Grays" under Col. C.W. Dupont, reserves under Col. J.J. Daniels, Col. Caraway Smith's cavalry, Maj. William H. Milton's troops, Capt. Pat Houstoun's artillery, Capt. Joseph L. Denham's artillery, active Capt. D.W. Cwynn and the West Florida Cadets (dubbed the "Baby Corps") commanded by Capt. V.M. Johnson.

The Baby Corps was a group of young men from the West Florida Seminary, known today as Florida State University. A monument at the battlefield notes that the corps consisted of boys "young as the youngest who wore the gray." By some accounts, the boys were so small, two of them could fit comfortably on a single horse.

Meanwhile, in Tallahassee citizens began construction of Ft. Houstoun on what was then the outskirts of the city, where the fort's earthworks still stand.

On March 5, the invaders began their advance, forcing Scott's men to fall back to Newport, but failed to cross the St. Marks River. Confederate commanders realized the invaders were attempting to make their way to Natural Bridge to cross there.

The gallantry of Lt. Col. Scott and his command delayed the march of the enemy (on March 4 and 5) giving time for reinforcements to arrive, Miller recalled.

Capt. Samuel Spencer left the fort at St. Marks in the evening of March 5 and reported to Miller at Newport that troops at the fort were preparing to blow up the structure and burn their gunboat *Spray*. Miller immediately headed to the fort and ordered the defenders there not to withdraw.

"I will hear no more of the abandonment of this strong position," Miller said, "and I will hold him a traitor who speaks again of the abandonment of this position, the key to the defense of Tallahassee."

The confederates took their positions at Natural Bridge on the morning of March 6.

"While the troops were being formed, the skirmishers were driven in and the enemy advanced at early dawn with the charge but were temporarily checked by a few charges of shell from Houstoun's battery," Miller said. "In the early dawn, the enemy advanced in force across the pass, firing rapidly, but were driven back by a mingled fire of musketry and canister."

The federals continued to fire small arms at the defenders while Miller's troops regrouped for the impending attack, and at 9 a.m., Denham arrived with three artillery pieces to complement the cannons already on line.

"During the whole morning until 11 o'clock, a desultory fire was kept up by the skirmishers on our front, and at 11 o'clock the enemy advanced in full force, and opened (fire) from his artillery," Miller wrote.

Union troops made four attempts to cross the pass where the river goes underground and forms a natural bridge, but confederates were positioned to concentrate their fire at the narrow spot and repeatedly beat back the invaders. Miller sensed that the invaders were about to retreat, and he ordered two companies to follow them – not to attack, but to report when the enemy had gone.

"...Although our men were footsore and weary, they marched that night through wet, stony ground..." Miller told the historical society. "I cannot too highly commend the spirit with which the militia, from boys of 14 to men of 70, from the humble woodsman to the highest civil dignitaries, came to the defense of their country and bore with patient endurance a long night's march. Their bravery needs no comment."

When the battle was over, Union casualties totaled 21 dead, 89 wounded and 38 missing. Confederate casualties were three dead and 22 wounded, none of them from the Baby Corps.

Victory belonged to Miller, but glory is a fleeting thing. Within a few weeks, the Confederacy succumbed to the Union, and the nation reunited.

It was time then for a badly scarred America to begin the healing and reconstruction that spawned the great country it is today.

Gov. Milton committed suicide at his home near Marianna.

Since then, wars have come and gone, and like all great cities, Tallahassee has never failed to send its sons and daughters to answer the country's call to arms. Still, not since March 6, 1865 has the horror of modern battle hovered over Tallahassee.

Peace and Healing

Death was the price of peace. The Old South had died from mortal wounds inflicted by Union cannons and rifles by the time Maj. Gen. Edward M. McCook arrived in Tallahassee on May 10, 1865. He came to accept the surrender of Confederate troops and all public property.

On McCook's arrival, Confederate Maj. Gen. Samuel Jones, commander of local forces, dutifully surrendered as he was obliged to do when further fighting was pointless.

Even the decisive Confederate victory two months earlier at Natural Bridge, near present-day Woodville, accomplished no more than to buy a little time. The war was lost. Dixie lay in ashes.

According to "The Surrender of Tallahassee," by James P. Jones and William Warren Rogers, published in the 1963-67 edition of *Apalachee*, McCook made a modest entrance into town. Although he had 300 crack cavalrymen at his disposal, he came alone except for his immediate staff. The main body of Union warriors approached at a leisurely pace from four miles to the north so as not to humiliate the defeated citizens of the Florida capital unnecessarily.

Jones and Rogers recounted that a terrified young boy screamed, "Yankees! Yankees!" startling the other children and adults who lined the street to observe as McCook made his way into town.

Tallahasseans knew the general was coming. Jones and Rogers reported in their account of the affair that there had been talk of emigration, and even of guerilla warfare, but when the time came, the surrender was peaceful.

"The general was very properly received by representative men of the place, and the courtesies due him were gracefully extended," recounted one young woman whose words were recorded in Ellen Call Long's *Florida Breezes*.

Another local woman, however, saw the yankees' arrival in a different light. Susan Bradford Eppes, in her book, *Through Some Eventful Years*, wrote: "McCook's men got us after all. About 12 o'clock today (May 11) they came in sight, a long line of blue. I don't know how I could ever have thought the blue uniform was pretty...They look ugly enough today."

The woman said her mother felt safe enough to bring her valuables out of hiding. "But I do not feel safe about myself or anything else," the young woman said.

Her account indicates that the Union officers maintained strict discipline among the troops at first, not allowing them to straggle or enter private enclosures. A few days later, she said, things changed.

Her report reads: "...some things in the Capitol were hidden away but, just as it is in case of a fire, the most valuable possessions were left behind and the first yankees who reached Tallahassee helped themselves. Well, it is what we expected."

Jones and Rogers wrote that most soldiers behaved themselves although some certainly did enter homes without invitation.

Confederate troops began to pour in to Tallahassee to surrender their arms and receive parole from the Union commander. Between 6,000 and 8,000 soldiers surrendered and turned over their 40 cannons, 2,500 small arms, 450 sabers, 1,618 bayonets and other items such as niter, pikes, lances, hospital supplies, horses, mules, cattle, bacon, salt, sugar, corn and flour.

Food was in short supply among the civilians, and McCook exchanged horses and mules that were unsuitable for military service for corn or forage. Later, he loaned food items to the people. McCook remarked that he found the citizenry and soldiers demonstrated "...only the most entire spirit of submission to my authority, and in the majority of instances an apparent cheerful acquiescence to the present order of things."

May 27, the *Florida Union* of Jacksonville reported that nearly all of Maj. Gen. Jones' men had been paroled and that large numbers of paroled Confederate soldiers were returning home from Carolina.

While Tallahasseans did not physically resist occupation, there was at least one incident that irritated McCook. The Reverand W.J. Ellis, rector of St. John's Episcopal Church, omitted the customary prayer for the president of the United States during a public ceremony.

"I thought it my duty to Christianize him," McCook said of his reaction to the incident, which he viewed as an act of defiance. McCook fired off a communique to the minister:

"Although it may be inconsistent with your personal feelings to offer

this prayer, yet as it is part of the formula prescribed by the bench of bishops, and as many who may probably hereafter worship with your congregation will desire the privilege of praying for their president, I must request that in the future you either include this customary prayer or the church be closed."

The ceremony ending the Confederacy in Tallahassee took place on May 20. Officials raised the Stars and Stripes over the Capitol as a gun sounded for every state in the Union. When the flag came down at sunset, 100 guns (perhaps as many as 200, according to one account) sounded in salute. The governor, state officials, a few citizens and newly-freed blacks stood by and observed. Even though they doubtlessly were humbled by defeat, many removed their hats out of respect.

By May 21, McCook's task was completed, and the time had come for reconstruction to begin. With the horrors of the Civil War behind them, Tallahasseans turned their attention to binding their wounds and to building a new community in a nation that was at last at peace.

War Mobilized the Women

The news reached Tallahassee on April 7, 1917. Congress had declared war.

"The effect was electrical," wrote a young woman, known to us only as Elizabeth. "I felt it in the quivering of my nerves, and I saw it in the faces around me."

The pages of *A Century of Tallahassee Girls, As Viewed From the Leaves of Their Diaries*, reveal the story of how the news changed Elizabeth's life and the lives of her classmates at the Florida State College for Women.

Back then, news bulletins drew crowds to the drug store at the corner of Monroe and College streets. Someone routinely posted them on the window there. For nearly three years, Tallahasseans had trekked to the drug store during the evenings to follow developments in the Great European War – later renamed World War I.

"Today, I am going to look around to see where I am needed most. Then down to business," Elizabeth wrote.

Three days later, she found her calling during her classes at the college.

"It doesn't sound very romantic after hearing the girls' plans to go as nurses, ambulance drivers and canteen workers," she confided to her diary. Another plan did appeal to her, however.

Elizabeth wrote that in dietetics class, a woman she identified as Miss Simms, chairman of the State Home Demonstration work, stepped in front of her desk and looked in the young women's faces. Then Miss Simms began to speak "slowly and deliberately, but with intense earnestness."

"Young ladies, I can read in your faces that you are very much awake to the present situation," Miss Simms said. "...Our allies are suffering more and more from the want of food, and we shall be called upon to perform more and more to relieve this condition."

Then there was a break in Miss Simms' voice.

"If we are to send a great army to Europe, you can readily see that the food question will be even more acute," Miss Simms said.

Miss Simms told the young women that America would produce the food, even if it had to use soldiers to till the soil, but preservation of food would require the help of every class in food study in the United States.

The same campus that had, in 1865, unleashed a company of young men and boys to drive away invaders in the Battle of Natural Bridge, called on its young women to do their part in a new war effort.

When Miss Simms asked how many would like to take part in the cause, "The whole class arose as one," Elizabeth wrote. "And that's the way I found my place."

It was a month later before Elizabeth found time to return to her diary.

"If ever there was a time I should record things, it's now," she wrote. "Well, I don't know whether I'm canned or dried or just plain pickled, but I'm sure it's one of the three."

Elizabeth wrote that she and the other young women labored from 6 a.m. to 6 p.m. daily, canning foods, working in the kitchen and trying out recipes from Washington and elsewhere.

When Miss Simms had learned of a shortage of cans, according to Elizabeth, the older woman borrowed $2,000 from a bank to secure a carload of cans. At least some of the cans were to be turned over to farmers and canning clubs, but the cost of crating, if men had to be hired, would add to the expense of the college women's efforts.

"Any suggestions?" Miss Simms asked.

"I don't see why we couldn't do (the crating too)," responded Elizabeth's classmate, Kate.

"My but I'm proud of you girls," Miss Simms said. "I thought I could depend upon you."

In groups of 10 or 12, the young women took time out from classes to board the trucks that carried them to the canning shop. They had stored the cans in a leaky old warehouse near the railroad station. Miss Simms, distressed by the clouds that had begun to form over town, had commented to Elizabeth and another young woman, Margaret, that rain might spill through the roof of the warehouse and ruin the cans.

"It was a fortunate remark, for at 12 o'clock, I was wakened by one of the most terrific rains I've ever heard," Elizabeth wrote.

Margaret also was alarmed and rushed into Elizabeth's room, saying she couldn't sleep for fear the cans would rust and be ruined. Other young women poured into the room, "with white-scared faces," fearing for the cans.

"We sat around in kimonos and screamed at each other above the noise of the storm," Elizabeth wrote. "About 2 o'clock the rain slowed down a bit, and someone suggested if it stopped by daylight, there was just one thing to do, to take cloths down there and dry out the cans."

One of the women, Sarah, volunteered to sit up and watch the weather and to call the others at 4 a.m. if the weather eased enough to permit the can salvage operation. The other young women gathered old cloths and tried to sleep. At 4 a.m. the call came, and 20 young women rushed through a breakfast of tea and crackers before scrambling to the warehouse.

"Day was just breaking as we swung down the muddy, slippery hill singing 'There's a long, long trail' and 'Pack up your troubles in your own kit bag and smile, smile, smile,'" Elizabeth wrote. "I tell you singing has carried us all through some mighty tight places."

At the station, the young women recruited the engineer of a waiting train to break down the door of the warehouse. Inside, they found their worst fears had been well-founded. Three-fourths of the cans had water in them.

The young women went to work with desperate determination.

At 8 a.m., Miss Simms and some of the other young women drove to the warehouse with a great pot of coffee and some rolls, and at noon, someone brought buckets of soup and cheese sandwiches. During the day, other young women came by to pitch in and relieve the exhausted crew.

By 6 p.m., every can was dry.

Elizabeth's diary doesn't mention how much food the young women canned in 1917, but in an Aug. 26, 1918 entry she recorded that the women had just completed the last of the fruits and vegetables before classes were to begin. In all, she said, the young women had filled 30,000 cans that year – most of it for the war effort and some for charity.

"And that's only the beginning," she wrote. "Next summer we'll do better if we have to start a factory."

As it turned out, the war ended a few weeks later, and the young women were able to refocus on their studies as peace settled over the world again.

Admittedly less famous than the Civil War's Battle of Natural Bridge in 1865, the World War I battle to provide food for America's warriors, earned the Florida State College for Women – now called Florida State University – a place of honor in the history of Florida and the history of the United States.

Part VI

The Twentieth Century

No Whistling Allowed

"At no time shall there be undue disturbance in the residence halls, such as running, calling from windows, whistling, or any like disorder," read the *Laws of Honor* which regulated student behavior at Florida State College for Women in 1927. Violations could result in a stiff penalty. It could run as high as a 25-cent fine...maybe even 50 cents.

The College Government Association published the rules in a handbook.

"The privileges of the individual must be subordinated to the rights of the community. Every student shall conduct herself at all times in such a way as to uphold her own good name and that of the college," said the *Laws of Honor* in laying out the rules.

Dancing was a matter that required well-defined boundaries. Members of the College Government Association were permitted to dance, but not with men on campus or in Tallahassee. No one was permitted to leave college to attend dances in nearby towns.

On the other hand, because of the warm relationship that existed then between the Florida State College for Women (FCW) and the men's college (known today as the University of Florida) the rules provided: "Students may go to Gainesville for the weekend to attend student dances provided a chaperon is with the party."

Smoking? Well, okay, but not for members of the College Government Association.

Everybody had to go to church on Sunday and to chapel four times a week. Also on Sundays, "...Students must conduct themselves so that they will not be conspicuous in the community and will not disturb others."

Students who wanted to make noise on Saturday, had to do it before noon. Afternoons and evenings were to be quiet so other students could study and rest.

"Social arrangements," of course, required specific rules.

"A student may make arrangement with the social director to walk to the theater, to luncheon, or to church with an escort, under the following conditions: (a.) Two students may go with two escorts. (b.) Two students may go with one escort.

But beware: "A student may not sit in a car with a man, either on campus or elsewhere." And: "Students are not expected to carry on extended conversations or to have treats with men when in town."

Oh yes...one more thing: "Students may not go to hotels in Tallahassee except with permission from the director of resident halls."

If a student needed to leave the campus over night, she was required to arrange it with the social director of the residence hall, and if the absence involved leaving Tallahassee, the student would have to arrange permission from her parent or guardian two days in advance. Failure to abide by the requirement, or failure to register accurately, made the student subject to a 50-cent fine.

If the student had to leave due to her own illness, that was different, but she had to make arrangements with the college physician before leaving.

On Sundays, the rules did allow students to go to the post office, telegraph office or tea rooms during the day, but they were not allowed to go to the drug store or cafes without special permission from the social director. They had to be back by 8 p.m.

Any situation wherein a student might find herself compromised required the presence of a chaperon. The rules required that chaperons could be faculty members, social directors or other persons designated by the dean of students. Anybody else would have to secure approval of the director of residence halls before serving as a chaperon. One exception: "Parents are always chaperons for their own daughters and for other students who have the permission of the social director to be included in the party."

A young man with a car was practically the devil in disguise. For a young lady to ride with one of them certainly required limits.

"Students may ride with young men by arranging with the social director. Students riding with young men must register on their date cards as having a social engagement."

Two students could ride to town with men in the daytime without chaperonage, provided they were signed up. At night, however, students had to have an approved chaperon, unless two students with escorts made arrangements with the social director and registered with the social director immediately upon returning. A 50-cent fine awaited those who failed to abide by this rule.

There was danger outside the security of the campus and safety was in numbers.

"For long hikes, or hiking on unfrequented roads, there must be a group of 10 people who remain as a group while on the hike."

Short hikes only required four people.

Other rules specified requirements for care of rooms, contacts with fraternities (at Gainesville, no doubt), swimming, dining room use, deliveries and entertainment functions.

Remarkably, the rules made no provision for a dress code – perhaps because the social pressures of the day dictated one that rendered a campus dress code unnecessary.

As we enter the 21st century, it's tempting to look back on the 1927 *Laws of Honor* as a silly set of rules that unfairly – and perhaps illegally – inhibited self-expression and creative growth among FCW's students. On the other hand, in 1927, FCW's student body might well have been horrified by the comparatively uninhibited conduct of Florida State University coeds of today.

Times were different in 1927. Attitudes were different. It was important back then that FCW students act like ladies and reflect credit on their college. If they didn't, the college's public image suffered, and that mattered.

Besides, only a lady could hope to find a husband among the gentlemen at Gainesville.

Shivering in Fear

Tallahassee shivered in fear in the opening days of 1978. A maniac was loose, and nobody knew who he was.

Even then-Sheriff Ken Katsaris warned frightened citizens, "Lock your doors, don't go out on the streets alone, and don't take chances."

It was about four hours before dawn on Jan.15 when Florida State University police arrived on the scene at the university's Chi Omega house, 661 S. Jefferson St. Four coeds had been clubbed mercilessly; two of them had been strangled and one or both of the fatalities had been raped -- all by an unknown intruder. Within 90 minutes, police learned another FSU woman, six blocks away in a 431 Dunwoody St. duplex, also had been clubbed and left for dead. She was one of the survivors.

Investigators revealed the identities of the victims as: sorority sisters Margaret Eliza Bowman, 21, of St. Petersburg; Lisa Levy, 20, of St. Petersburg; Karen Chandler, 21, of Tallahassee; and Kathy Kleiner, 19 of Miami in addition to the Dunwoody Street woman, Cheryl Ann Thomas, 21, of Richmond, Va. Ms. Bowman and Ms. Levy did not survive.

Fortunately for investigators, another Chi Omega member, Nita Jane Neary had seen the killer leave the building at 3:26 a.m. She described him to police as a white male, in his early 20s, 5-foot-8 to 5-foot-10, and weighing 155-160 pounds.

About 40 other women had slept through the attacks at the Chi Omega house, unaware of what had happened until awakened by the weeping and terrified voices of their sorority sisters.

Authorities posted heavy guards at Tallahassee Memorial Hospital to protect the survivors while investigators waited to question them.

By early afternoon, Sorority Row residents still waited nearby for somebody to tell them what had happened down the street. The university sent Claudia Grace, assistant director of activities, to brief them.

"We have a deranged murderer on our hands, a crazy man," she said.

"We don't know where he is, why he is doing it, what he will do next....We just want you to be more cautious than you have ever been."

Students scrambled for telephones to assure parents they weren't among the victims. Some could only sob.

The *Tallahassee Democrat* quoted an unidentified Centel switchboard operator as saying long-distance switchboards "lit up like a Christmas tree."

Police released information that two fraternities and four sororities had been burglarized during the lengthy Christmas vacation and that they already had begun lecturing at each house in an effort to encourage tighter security.

Student government President Doug Guetzloe announced that he would renew his plan for a $12,500 student patrol, a plan that had been vetoed six months earlier by the Student Senate.

Coeds began moving out of their campus residences to move in with friends or relatives. The campus escort service, manned by fraternity members, saw its normal workload of four or fewer calls per night jump to 60 after the murders.

By Jan. 18, 12 students had withdrawn from classes.

Then the predictable flood of rumors began. One rumor was that police already had staked out the Chi Omega house before the murders in an anti-burglary operation.

"Not true," police said.

Another rumor was that a sixth victim had been discovered in bushes near Doak Campbell Stadium.

"Not true," Katsaris said.

Still another rumor was that the previous May, another Chi Omega sister, Linda Sue Thompson, had been clubbed in the back of the head at Dorman Hall late one night and taken to a wooded area and left for dead.

"True, although not firmly linked to the murders," investigators said.

A task force of 40 investigators was working the case two weeks after the murders. By Jan. 24, police had questioned 44 possible suspects.

Nothing.

The task force dwindled to 13 by the end of the month.

Newspaper accounts reported some frightened students were carrying weapons; faulty locks were undergoing repairs; hysteria blanketed Tallahassee.

It was Feb. 15 before officers received a break in the case. A Pensacola policeman, David Lee, had spotted a suspicious vehicle, driving slowly through an alley behind some businesses in that city at 1:30 a.m. and followed the orange Volkswagen to investigate.

When Lee notified his dispatcher of the vehicle's tag number, the report came back that the car had been reported stolen in Tallahassee.

Lee pulled the vehicle over and drew his gun.

While Lee attempted to handcuff the young suspect, the suspect ran, and the dangling handcuffs looked like a gun, so the officer opened fire. The sounds of gunfire halted the suspect and the officer took him into custody.

At first, the suspect identified himself as Kenneth Misner, a member of the FSU track team. He had Misner's drivers license and duplicate copies of Misner's diploma and birth certificate. He also had various credit cards and other identification bearing other names.

"I stole them in Tallahassee," he told police.

The next day, the suspect dropped the claim that he was Misner, and assumed the name "John Doe," pending a conference with an attorney. He then made a series of calls that enabled police to identify him as Theodore "Ted" Bundy.

In an interview that courts later was ruled inadmissable as evidence, Bundy implied to investigators that he had been on a murder spree that had spanned six states. Investigative reporters that have since written about Bundy have concluded that his victims – nearly all brunettes with long hair, parted in the middle – may have totaled three dozen or more.

Eventually, Ted Bundy was convicted and sentenced to death in Florida's electric chair for the Chi Omega murders and another murder of a pretty 12-year-old Lake City girl.

The state carried out the sentence Jan. 24, 1989.

Even now, thousands of Tallahasseans shudder to recall that awful day when fear blanketed this city.

Some like Gary Robertson remember Bundy's confident demeanor as the killer purchased a bicycle from him with a credit card that turned out to be stolen. Some like Cherie Barrineau – an attractive brunette with long hair, parted in the middle back in 1978 – tremble to think what might have happened to her if Lee had not put a stop to the killing. Bundy had Ms. Barrineau's driver's license with him when he was arrested. She didn't even know it was missing until police contacted her about it.

During the centuries that people have lived at the site now known as Tallahassee, many great disasters have come and gone, but nothing else in modern times has shaken the community like the senseless Chi Omega murders of 1978.

The execution of Ted Bundy left Tallahassee with a feeling that, at last, the danger had passed. Still, Tallahassee will never again be the city it was before the terrible morning of Jan. 15, 1978.

Epilogue

As the author, allow me to be the first to acknowledge that too many chapters are missing from this book. The history of Tallahassee holds far more stories of courage, perseverence and tragedy than these few pages can reveal, but hopefully, this work was a modest start. Forgive me, dear reader, for failing to tell the whole story of Tallahassee, and join me in celebrating the morsels of history that compose this book. Perhaps you can fill in some of the gaping holes that escaped the press in this feeble attempt to explain why we are here, and why we claim the right to be so proud of our city.

Tallahassee has seen its days of triumph and its hours of defeat. It has survived since long before the European explorers discovered it. Tallahassee draws strength from its people and inspiration from its past. Since 1845, Tallahassee has been the capital of a great state, cradling its government, reflecting the character of its people and charting its future.

Our hope is that centuries from now some scholar will research the care and feeding of Tallahassee during our watch and will conclude that those of us who live here now have somehow expanded the legacy begun by those who called Tallahassee home before we arrived.

List of References

Hernando De Soto and the Indians of Florida, Jerald Malanich and Charles Hudson, University Press of Florida, Gainesville, Florida, 1993.

Apalachee, the Land Between the Rivers, Dr. John Hann, University Press of Florida, Gainesville, Florida, 1988.

The Search for the Missing Wakulla (Oops! Jefferson) Volcano, Sonny (the Round Man) Branch and J. Rob, The Skeeterville Press, Tallahassee, Florida, 1995.

Florida Breezes, Ellen Call Long, University of Florida Press, Gainesville, Florida, 1893.

Ante-Bellum Tallahassee, Bertram H. Groene, Florida Heritage Foundation, Tallahassee, Florida, 1981.

The Other Florida, Gloria Jahoda, Valentine Books, Port Salerno, Florida, 1978.

God Willing: A History of St. John's Episcopal Church, Carl Stauffer, The Church, Tallahassee, Florida, 1984.

History of St. John's Church, Tallahassee, The Reverend W.H. Carter, Appendix C, Historical Papers and Journal of Semi-Centennial of the Church in Florida, January 18-19, 1888.

A Century of Tallahassee Girls, as Viewed From the Leaves of Their Diaries, Clara R. Hayden, Foote & Davies, Atlanta, Georgia, 1924.

"Tallahassee and the 1841 Yellow Fever Epidemic," Barbara Miller, *Apalachee*, Vol. 8 1971-1979, Tallahassee Historical Society, Tallahassee, Florida, 1978.

Tallahassee, Favored Land, Mary Louise Ellis, William Warren Rogers and Joan Morris, Donning, Norfolk, Virginia, 1988.

"The Tallahassee Fire of 1843," Fred Ley, Jr., *Apalachee*, 1948-1950, Tallahassee Historical Society, Tallahassee, Florida, 1950.

"The Corporation of Tallahassee, 1826-1860," Dorothy Dodd, *Apalachee*, 1948-1950, Tallahassee Historical Society, Tallahassee, Florida, 1950.

"Ring Tournaments in Tallahassee," William G. Dodd, *Apalachee*, 1948-1950, Tallahassee Historical Society, Tallahassee, Florida, 1950.

"Social Aspects of Leon County Wills and Inventories 1826-1845," Arthur R. Seymour, *Apalachee, 1948-1950*, Tallahassee Historical Society, Tallahassee, Florida, 1950.

"The Proctors — Antonio, George and John," Rosalind Parker, *Apalachee*, 1946, Tallahassee Historical Society, Tallahassee, Florida, 1946.

Tales of Tallahassee, Twice Told and Untold, James R. Knott, limited edition by the author, 1995.

History of Florida, Charlton W. Tebeau, University of Miami Press, Coral Gables, Florida, 1971.

The Florida Handbook, Allen Morris, Peninsular Publishing Co., Tallahassee, Florida, 1991.

Florida, a Short History, Dr. Michael Gannon, University Press of Florida, Gainesville, Florida, 1993.

An address to the Tallahassee Historical Society, Brig. Gen. William Miller, 1901, posthumously presented by Mark F. Boyd, *Apalachee*, Vol.4, 1950-1956, Tallahassee Historical Society, Tallahassee, Florida, 1956.

"The Surrender of Tallahassee," James P. Jones and William Warren Rogers, *Apalachee*, Vol. 6, 1963-1967, Tallahassee Historical Society, Tallahassee, Florida, 1967.

Through Some Eventful Years, Susan Bradford Eppes, University of Florida Press, Gainesville, Florida, 1968.

Laws of Honor, student handbook, Florida State College for Women, College Government Association, Tallahassee, Florida, 1927.

Daily news coverage and commentaries, James Cramer, Deanna Thompson, Michael Whiteley, Pat Harbolt, Ed Hardee, Ellen Templeton, Tom Shroder, Seth Effron, Mike Abrams, Malcolm B. Johnson, Rich Oppel, Hettie Cobb and William Nottingham, *Tallahassee Democrat*, Tallahassee, Florida, January 16-31, 1978.

About the Author

Henry Cabbage is a native Floridian, born and reared (off and on) in Panama City. Trained as a journalist, he worked 10 years as a newspaper reporter and radio newscaster before moving to Tallahassee in 1984.

Cabbage has always maintained an abiding love for the history of Florida, particularly north Florida. His words appear regularly in newspapers and magazines across Florida and other southeastern states.

He is currently the public information director of Florida's state wildlife agency and a freelance writer. He resides in Tallahassee with his wife Joan.